The Future of the Internet

Other books in the At Issue series:

At ✳ Issue

The Future of the Internet

Tom Head, *Book Editor*

Bruce Glassman, *Vice President*
Bonnie Szumski, *Publisher*
Helen Cothran, *Managing Editor*

GREENHAVEN PRESS
An imprint of Thomson Gale, a part of The Thomson Corporation

THOMSON
™
GALE

Detroit • New York • San Francisco • San Diego • New Haven, Conn.
Waterville, Maine • London • Munich

For more information, contact
Greenhaven Press
27500 Drake Rd.
Farmington Hills, MI 48331-3535
Or you can visit our Internet site at http://www.gale.com

LIBRARY OF CONGRESS CATALOGING-IN-PUBLICATION DATA
The future of the internet / Tom Head, book editor.
p. cm. — (At issue)
Includes bibliographical references and index.
ISBN 0-7377-2713-6 (lib. : alk. paper) — ISBN 0-7377-2714-4 (pbk. : alk. paper)
1. Information society. 2. Internet—Social aspects. I. Head, Tom. II. At issue (San Diego, Calif.)
HM851.F88 2005
303.45'33—dc22   2004060713

Printed in the United States of America

Contents

Introduction

"It is with a feeling of humbleness," the executive said, "that I come to this moment of announcing the birth in this country of a new art so important in its implications that it is bound to affect all society. It is an art which shines like a torch of hope in a troubled world. It is a creative force which we must learn to utilize for the benefit of all mankind." The executive was RCA's David Sarnoff, the new creative force was television, and the year was 1939.

The development of television and the Internet are strikingly similar. Both technologies began as novelties that only scientists, government officials, and a few privileged hobbyists were familiar with. Both have been alternately perceived as conduits to a perfect future or portals to a nightmarish hell. Still under development, their future untold, their ultimate influence unclear, both exist today squarely within the mainstream of human culture. Still, with a fifty-year head start the history of television may provide some indication of what the future of the Internet will be like.

On April 30, 1939, the New York World's Fair opened its doors and invited visitors to attend the World of Tomorrow exhibit. Inside were amazing wonders: the time capsule (to be opened in the year 6939), the first long-distance telephone call, the first nylon stockings, a primitive fax machine, and General Motors' amazing Futurama exhibit, which promised automated highways and massive suburban utopias. In the midst of these wonders was a new device that visitors could actually purchase: the television.

It certainly was not the first television. Russian scientists Boris Rosing and Vladimir Zworykin invented the prototype television sometime between 1907 and 1910, and the British Broadcasting Corporation (BBC) began broadcasting television programs in 1932. But the early televisions were expensive, displayed low-quality video, and—perhaps most important of all—lacked access to local stations that broadcast television content. It was not until the 1939 World's Fair that clear, "high-definition" television was introduced. The cabinet-sized boxes,

6

with screens tiny by modern standards—the largest screen, on a set that sold for about six thousand dollars in modern currency, was about seven inches tall and nine inches wide—were actually suitable for home use, and the U.S.-based National Broadcasting Company (NBC) immediately promised twenty-five hours per week of television content. Although it would be decades before a majority of Americans owned television sets, the age of television had begun.

The new medium sparked admiration in some and criticism in others. For many it evoked doomsday prophecies. Many analysts echoed RCA's David Sarnoff, believing that television would become a cure-all for human ills. Others argued that the new technology would lead to an irrevocable cultural decline. U.S. Federal Communications Commission (FCC) chair Newton Minow complained in 1961,

> When television is good, nothing—not the theater, not the magazines or newspapers—nothing is better. But when television is bad, nothing is worse. I invite you to sit down in front of your television set when your station goes on the air and stay there without a book, magazine, [or] newspaper . . . to distract you—and keep your eyes glued to that set until the station signs off. I can assure you that you will observe a vast wasteland.

Other analysts feared that the technology would provide a way for governments to spy on their citizens. In his 1948 novel *1984*, British journalist George Orwell portrayed a hellish world controlled by a totalitarian government that used television screens to monitor its people.

The development of the Internet followed a similar course. Like television, the technology was first used only by a handful of people and was not user-friendly. In 1961 MIT professor J.C.R. Licklider proposed a "galactic network" linking computers worldwide. The computers of 1962 were unreliable, extremely primitive by contemporary standards, took up entire rooms, and were prohibitively expensive. As a result, their use was largely limited to governments and major corporations. Governments were interested in a type of galactic network in order to share data. The Advanced Research Projects Agency Network (ARPANET) went online in November 1969 and allowed government computers to communicate with one another. In 1984 the U.S. military established a separate network

(MILNET) to distribute unclassified information between military bases, and in 1986 the nonprofit National Science Foundation established NSFNET so that scientists could use computers to network and share information. The U.S. government shut down ARPANET in 1989, and private organizations took over responsibility for international computer networking. The modern Internet was born.

Since then the Internet has captured the public's imagination at least as much as television did. Box office science fiction epics such as *The Terminator* and *The Matrix* tell of a world oppressed by an Internet that has grown too powerful for its human users. Mainstream suspense thrillers such as *The Net* and even horror films like *fear dot com* also call attention to the hazards of the Internet, particularly the risks it poses to individual privacy. A writer for the *Chronicle of Higher Education* gave a new version of the FCC's "vast wasteland" speech in an April 1997 article, writing that "the Internet is a shallow and unreliable electronic depository of dirty pictures, inaccurate rumors, bad spelling and worse grammar, inhabited largely by people with no demonstrable social skills."

While some saw the Internet as the latest version of Orwell's telescreen, others saw the medium as a conduit to Utopia. John Perry Barlow's "Declaration of the Independence of Cyberspace" sets out a defense of what he regards as the basic principles behind Internet culture. He argues that cyberspace, because it is devoid of geographical boundaries, promotes democracy and equality:

> Cyberspace consists of transactions, relationships, and thought itself, arrayed like a standing wave in the web of our communications. Ours is a world that is both everywhere and nowhere, but it is not where bodies live. We are creating a world that all may enter without privilege or prejudice accorded by race, economic power, military force, or station of birth. . . . They are all based on matter, and there is no matter here.

To be sure, both television and the Internet have elicited fanciful prophecies such as this. Both began as primitive technologies and quickly evolved into complex communications media that now exist at the center of human culture. The parallels between these technologies invite observers to view the history of television as instructive of what the future of the Internet might be. While optimists thought television would cure all of society's ills and doomsayers predicted that it would lead to humanity's downfall, neither turned out to be right. Many predict the same will hold true for the Internet: It will be neither as beneficial nor as harmful as people think. These analysts do not believe that the Internet will transform society into an egalitarian Eden or that it will lead to an irreversible decline in human societies. If television is any indication, they say, the Internet will both enhance and harm human societies but by a degree far more moderate than reactionary commentators predict.

The emergence of new technologies has always been accompanied by optimistic prophecies and doomsday predictions, and the Internet has been no exception. Although the history of television provides clues about how cyberspace will shape human societies in the years to come, only time will tell whether predictions about the future of the Internet will turn out to be true.

1

The Internet Will Enhance Human Life

Joseph H. Coates

Joseph H. Coates founded Coates & Jarratt, Inc., a consulting firm that has advised businesses on possible future developments for over twenty-five years. He is author or coauthor of four books dealing with the future and coedited the Encyclopedia of the Future.

The further integration of the Internet with other technologies such as television will radically change society over the next fifteen to twenty years. Internet shopping will make mail-order shopping largely obsolete. It will improve relations between organized labor unions and corporations. The Internet will also allow users to participate, at any distance, in social events. Through technologies such as the Global Positioning System (GPS), it will make users effortlessly aware of where they are and help them to find whatever they need at all times. In addition, it will make driving safer, medicine more effective, and travel both less necessary and more enjoyable. In these ways and in many others the Internet will transform global culture and significantly improve quality of life.

> "Despite the dot-com meltdown, we found that the Internet is more vigorous than ever; a large majority of Americans go online, Internet use continues and growing numbers of non-users expect to go online in the next year."
> ——Jeff Cole, director of the UCLA Center for Communication Policy

Through a series of scientific, technological, and business co-incidences, the evolution of information technology has led to a disjointed, competitive, and piecemeal communications system.

The telegraph, telephone, and radio resulted from separate inventions, each converted into businesses by people with different objectives. Television came about as a spin-off from radio to compete with film. About 30 years ago the latest technological marvel, the Internet, was dropped into the middle of this communications chaos.

Unlike anything that came before, the Internet was free, or nearly so, in the minds of the early user. It featured video screens, computer keyboards, and communication to anyone, anywhere in the world, who was part of the Internet network. It has become increasingly sophisticated in quality and reliability, more convenient to use, and immeasurably more popular and valuable with the creation of the World Wide Web. Its democratic feature—open to anyone, anonymously, if you choose—was most appealing.

Considering the Future

Looking ahead 15 to 20 years, the Internet will be unrecognizable. The rest of the telecommunications industry will also be unrecognizable as we approach the goal of universal, seamless communication from anyplace to anyplace, at any time.

Technological integration will be required through patchwork arrangements, either voluntarily or by government intervention. Businesses may evolve in an intelligent way to assume more and more of the total information package needed to serve all customers. . . .

Looking ahead 15 to 20 years, the Internet will be unrecognizable.

On the technological side, the biggest thing affecting the future of the Internet, aside from the integration of media, is the emergence of wireless telecommunications. The new third-generation wireless service in the United States has enough broad-bandwidth capacity to service the Internet. Broadband means the capacity to speedily carry voice, text, photographs, graphics, movement, and interaction.

Wireless Internet will become as familiar as wireline Internet, with which it will be seamlessly integrated. Continual decreasing computer size, declining cost, and increasing numbers of users worldwide will define the total emerging system. Broad-bandwidth imaging and interacting capabilities will have consequences in two categories.

> *Despite exaggerated expectations, Internet shopping is enormously successful.*

Some repercussions will develop truly new applications. One category is already existing applications that are substantially enhanced or expanded. Let's look at a number of these and see where they are going. Keep in mind that if costs drop as technology becomes more familiar and commonplace, it will expand the range of people, organizations, and institutions that will be on the system. As Internet pioneer Robert Metcalfe proposed years ago, the value of a network increases geometrically as the square of the number of people on the network.

Business Uses

Shopping by Internet is now widespread, in competition with catalog buying or visiting the mall. It is especially attractive where there is no shop, supplier, or boutique nearby. Despite exaggerated expectations, Internet shopping is enormously successful. As the quality of images and the capability of interaction grow, the Net will be the big challenge to catalogs, which derive their strength from small size, convenience, and use of color.

The Internet will allow you to see yourself, having sent a picture and your measurements to a vendor. If you are buying clothes, you will be able to examine a wide range of outfits, and place an order without ever leaving your chair, desk, or plane seat. You will be able to see yourself walking, sitting, or rotated at various angles in your outfits. (Some people will always want to shop traditionally because that is recreation for them.)

As with most new uses, it will not be either-or but will offer a widening of choices based on people's preferences and short-term pressures. Comparison shopping will be a cinch on the Internet and will drive down prices. Business-to-business network commerce is already flourishing and will expand tremendously. Auctions and various forms of bidding are already common and will become ubiquitous.

One consequence of Internet-based purchasing will be a radical change in logistics regarding the shipping of goods. As more things in smaller or larger packages are delivered to homes, offices, and business facilities, trucks themselves will change. The big ones will still be necessary, but there will be a lot more midsize and smaller ones to wend their way through the neighborhoods.

Some communities may resort to the Tokyo system, in which people place and pick up their Internet orders at a local chain, like 7-Eleven. The reason is that in Tokyo the street naming is so complex that it would be too expensive to deliver to individual addresses.

Wireline and wireless will help business operate not only around the clock but around the world, in the sense that any element of the business personnel or unit can contact any other element, anytime and anywhere. Out of that capability will come enhanced efficiency and effectiveness, tighter management, or looser reins where that is appropriate.

There will be more interpersonal action between people who are now normally distant. Groupware, the ability of multiple locations to simultaneously communicate, exchange ideas, discuss matters, and work on projects, will be a cohesive factor in global business.

> // Some markets will shrivel and even wither away. . . . Examples include travel agents, financial service advisers, and automobile dealers. //

On the other hand, we will develop an etiquette that will be a constraint on who has the right to contact whom, when, for what purpose, and under what circumstances. After all, the system could easily drive everyone to a frazzle without proper protocol. Small businesses will benefit; the global Internet will allow any size enterprise to market worldwide and find (or be found by) members of niche markets.

Emergence of Cyberunions

Some markets will shrivel and even wither away when it is cheaper, faster, and more reliable to do a task yourself. Examples include travel agents, financial service advisers, and automobile dealers. Their individual survival will depend on innovations in customer service.

Arthur Shostak, a longtime student of organized labor, foresees the emergence of cyberunions. The Internet will not just improve the old tools of unionism but will open up new levels of excellence, making strategic planning more feasible, flexible, and practical. As unions gain international breadth, their actions will become more sophisticated.

> *We might have wrist TVs, from the size of a wristwatch face up, to anything that will be comfortable on your forearm.*

In negotiations, if unions are able to call up the same in-depth information about the firm available to the employer, this will make solutions more mutually significant. The Internet will also allow unions to become more collegial, restoring the socialization and important interpersonal linkages that are so important to group cohesion and action.

Paralleling the new business-union relations will be public interest groups and nongovernmental organizations dealing with national or international governing bodies. The ability to gather, collect, process, and deliver information in depth and on demand during a negotiation or discussion will change relationships. The ability to confront solid information with solid information will reduce hostile confrontations. In almost all interorganizational negotiations, the best route is establishing cooperation on as much common ground as possible.

Surveys and panel voting will be common. Most promising will be real-time voting during TV programs on individual characters, acts, sequences, and outcomes. The questionable judgments of those who manage the media may be replaced by the more practical and down-to-earth judgments of viewers.

A surprisingly high percentage of people require supervision, whether as a condition of parole or for medical reasons.

The availability of wireless-bandwidth capabilities will make it practical to have two-way audio, video, and data communication with them, ensuring that they remain law-abiding, safe, and healthy. The Internet will be able to identify where people are, remind them of what they must do—take a pill, exercise—and where they must go, and verify the safety of those who are at risk.

There will be a great deal more interaction through wireless Internet as the devices shrink in size and capacity grows. We might have wrist TVs, from the size of a wristwatch face up, to anything that will be comfortable on your forearm.

[The September 11, 2001, terrorist attacks] have reminded all of us that oral communication is invaluable in an emergency. We will add to that the capability of imagery, which will be a primary improvement in dealing with physical, medical, social, occupational, or traffic emergencies. In a disaster, a picture will be invaluable in allocating resources, mobilizing, setting priorities, and managing rescue workers.

Contacting the Best Coach

When you take part in sports and recreation using the Internet, you will be able to have outstanding coaches watch you swing the club, toss the caber, or race the horse. The ability to have expert knowledge brought to a sports activity without the tremendous burden of cost and time will open up new capabilities to enhance individual performance. A related benefit will be the correction of potentially dangerous patterns or maneuvers that occur in every sport.

The Internet developed in the United States as if all the world spoke English and will do so forever.

The Internet will lead to public voting on sports in real time to conjecture on the next move, as the rugby or football team moves into action. Fox TV used this technology during [a] recent Super Bowl, when it asked fans to submit answers to upcoming plays by the Patriots and Rams. Instant display of results will add an exciting element to watching sports. Other kinds of recreation will be opened up by wireless devices: tiny cameras will allow us to see what a snorkeler sees, or to view the face of a person bungee jumping or driving a race car.

The Internet can be a factor in automobile safety. Some 42,000 people die each year in traffic accidents in the United States. The most dangerous drivers are the young and the elderly. Technology will provide real-time monitoring of their performance, reporting to the driver vocally while driving ("You took that turn too fast," "You are closing too quickly," or "You are delaying too long in applying the brakes").

> *You will not need to know the name of a building since GPS, the Global Positioning Satellite system, will automatically take care of that.*

Real-time reporting can become a combination of training and monitoring for young drivers and a refresher course and safety device for older drivers, who have slower responses. The feedback could be sent to your parents by Internet, or it could be replayed in the evening when you return home. For those with questionable driving records, monitoring could be mandated as a condition for maintaining one's license, with feedback continually sent to the traffic department.

Using a New Language—RUOK?

The Internet developed in the United States as if all the world spoke English and will do so forever. This is far from the truth, although English will be the dominant language for the English-speaking nations, most professionals, and big businesses.

Communications among multinational corporations and their principal suppliers will be in English. But when one gets down to the nitty-gritty, consumers' side of life, it seems unlikely that people who speak Turkish or Polish will search for and buy a washing machine using English rather than their native tongue.

A large expansion in new languages on the Internet is already under way. Keyboards will become more complex. In his book *Alpha Beta*, [author] John Man points out that there is a universal Unicode, which stores 143 characters to represent the alphabets in all languages. Complex graphic languages such as Arabic will have keyboards that can be flipped back and forth between the local language and English.

The Chinese will use a Roman keyboard for email, using a script called Pinyin, which converts the sounds of Chinese into Roman letters. The system can even take into account the tonal differences that are so important in Chinese.

The lexicographer David Crystal claims that Netspeak is emerging as a third form of communication, the other two types presumably being speech and text. The Internet will steadily change our ideas of grammar, syntax, and vocabulary. With regard to it, RUOK ["are you okay"]?

Medicine is a favorite subject for discussions on the Internet now. New uses will offer a combination of speed and flexibility of response to an accident, disaster, or individual patients. The ability to incorporate broad-bandwidth imaging and interaction will allow the practitioner to examine and diagnose the patient at a distance. Routine data gathering and monitoring of patients will be transmitted to the physicians' database.

> *The Internet will allow you to participate remotely in celebrations, weddings, births, and funerals as you interact with other people through life-size wall screens.*

A wireless Internet will transform sightseeing, eliminating the need to carry heavy guidebooks. It will allow you to call up anything you want, with the right level of detail to satisfy your needs.

You will not need to know the name of a building since GPS, the Global Positioning Satellite system, will automatically take care of that. The Internet will facilitate getting around in strange cities, minimizing the possibility of getting lost with no ready way of calling for help.

Taking Care of Home

The Internet will be the core of the most important information-technology development in the home, the electronic home work-study center. It will bring together all of the information technologies connected with the house and all of their functions: work at home, entertainment, recreation, and socialization.

A typical home will have seven or eight flat screens. The kitchen appliances will be connected to each other and networked to the Internet, allowing you to instruct them remotely from another room, your car, or your office. The ability to communicate internally with wireless will cost less than rewiring your house. Safety and security will cease to be concerns of the middle class and wealthy. The smart house will alert one to the presence of intruders, photograph them, and even capture them physically in many circumstances. The Internet will retain all the information it automatically sends to the police or fire department.

The Internet will allow you to participate remotely in celebrations, weddings, births, and funerals as you interact with other people through life-size wall screens. It will be the closest thing to being at the event, which may be 15 or 5,000 miles away.

The Internet will bring familiar forms of recreation into the home, but it will also lead to new types of entertainment and recreation. Socially, your contacts may be briefer but their numbers will be greater, and, on average, each will give satisfaction greater than you ever experienced before.

The boundless credible expectations of the Internet will enhance our lives, improve our work, free up our time, expand our contacts, and give most of us greater satisfaction in our activities.

2

The Emerging Wireless Internet Will Both Improve and Degrade Human Life

Howard Rheingold

Professional freelance writer and speaker Howard Rheingold writes the column Tomorrow, *which is syndicated worldwide. He is also author or coauthor of eleven books, including* Smart Mobs: The Next Social Revolution *(2002), from which this excerpt is taken.*

The use of mobile Internet devices has increased considerably in recent years. Soon, Internet-capable mobile devices will outnumber personal computers. As mobile technology grows more sophisticated, the Internet will rely less on desktop computers and more on small, inexpensive portable devices that everyone carries. In the future anyone carrying a state-of-the-art networked mobile device will be able to join a "smart mob" made up of countless other networked mobile devices, making it easy for anyone to instantly communicate with others. This social network also has a downside; such technology makes it easier for governments to spy on citizens and for terrorists and criminals to plan their activities.

The first signs of the next shift began to reveal themselves to me on a spring afternoon in the year 2000. That was when I began to notice people on the streets of Tokyo staring at their

Howard Rheingold, *Smart Mobs: The Next Social Revolution*. New York: Basic Books, 2002. Copyright © 2003 by Howard Rheingold. All rights reserved. Reprinted by permission of Perseus Books PLC, a member of Perseus Books, L.L.C.

mobile phones instead of talking to them. The sight of this behavior, now commonplace in much of the world, triggered a
sensation I had experienced a few times before—the instant
recognition that a technology is going to change my life in ways
I can scarcely imagine. Since then the practice of exchanging
short text messages via mobile telephones has led to the erup-
tion of subcultures in Europe and Asia. At least one government
has fallen, in part because of the way people used text messaging. Adolescent mating rituals, political activism, and corporate
management styles have mutated in unexpected ways.

I've learned that "texting," as it has come to be called, is
only a small harbinger of more profound changes to come over
the next ten years. My media moment at Shibuya Crossing was
only my first encounter with a phenomenon I've come to call
"smart mobs." When I learned to recognize the signs, I began to
see them everywhere—from barcodes to electronic bridge tolls.

The other pieces of the puzzle are all around us now but
haven't joined together yet. The radio chips designed to replace
barcodes on manufactured objects are part of it. Wireless Internet nodes in cafes, hotels, and neighborhoods are part of it.
Millions of people who lend their computers to the search for
extraterrestrial intelligence are part of it. The way buyers and
sellers rate each other on the Internet auction site eBay is part
of it. At least one key global business question is part of it: Why
is the Japanese company DoCoMo profiting from enhanced
wireless Internet services while U.S. and European mobile telephone operators struggle to avoid failure?

> *At least one government has fallen, in part because of the way people used text messaging.*

When you piece together these different technological, economic, and social components, the result is an infrastructure
that makes certain kinds of human actions possible that were
never possible before. The "killer apps" of tomorrow's mobile
infocom industry won't be hardware devices or software programs but social practices. The most far-reaching changes will
come, as they often do, from the kinds of relationships, enterprises, communities, and markets that the infrastructure makes
possible.

The Wireless Net

Smart mobs consist of people who are able to act in concert even if they don't know each other. The people who make up smart mobs cooperate in ways never before possible because they carry devices that possess both communication and computing capabilities. Their mobile devices connect them with other information devices in the environment as well as with other people's telephones. Dirt-cheap microprocessors are beginning to permeate furniture, buildings, and neighborhoods; products, including everything from box tops to shoes, are embedded with invisible intercommunicating smartifacts. When they connect the tangible objects and places of our daily lives with the Internet, handheld communication media mutate into wearable remote-control devices for the physical world.

> *The 'killer apps' of tomorrow's mobile infocom industry won't be hardware devices or software programs but social practices.*

Within a decade, the major population centers of the planet will be saturated with trillions of microchips, some of them tiny computers, many of them capable of communicating with each other. Some of these devices will be telephones, and they will also be supercomputers with the processing power that only the Department of Defense could muster a couple of decades ago. Some devices will read barcodes and send and receive messages to radio-frequency identity tags. Some will furnish wireless, always-on Internet connections and will contain global positioning devices. As a result, large numbers of people in industrial nations will have a device with them most of the time that will enable them to link objects, places, and people to online content and processes. Point your device at a street sign, announce where you want to go, and follow the animated map beamed to the box in your palm, or point at a book in a store and see what the *Times* and your neighborhood reading group have to say about it. Click on a restaurant and warn your friends that the service has deteriorated.

These devices will help people coordinate actions with others around the world—and, perhaps more importantly, with people nearby. Groups of people using these tools will gain new forms of social power, new ways to organize their interactions and exchanges just in time and just in place. Tomorrow's fortunes will be made by the businesses that find a way to profit from these changes, and yesterday's fortunes are already being lost by businesses that don't understand them. As with the personal computer and the Internet, key breakthroughs won't come from established industry leaders but from the fringes, from skunkworks and startups and even associations of amateurs. *Especially* associations of amateurs.

> **❝** *Within a decade, the major population centers of the planet will be saturated with trillions of microchips . . . many of them capable of communicating with each other.* **❞**

Although it will take a decade to ramp up, mobile communications and pervasive computing technologies, together with social contacts that were never possible before, are already beginning to change the way people meet, mate, work, fight, buy, sell, govern, and create. Some of these changes are beneficial and empowering, and some amplify the capabilities of people whose intentions are malignant. Large numbers of small groups, using the new media to their individual benefit, will create emergent effects that will nourish some existing institutions and ways of life and dissolve others. Contradictory and simultaneous effects are likely: People might gain new powers at the same time we lose old freedoms. New public goods could become possible, and older public goods might disappear.

When I started looking into mobile telephone use in Tokyo, I discovered that Shibuya Crossing was the most mobile-phone-dense neighborhood in the world: 80 percent of the 1,500 people who traverse that madcap plaza at each light change carry a mobile phone. I took that coincidence as evidence that I was on the right track, although I had only an inkling of how to define what I was tracking. It had not yet become clear to me that I was no longer looking for intriguing evidence about changing techno-social practices, but galloping off on a worldwide hunt for the shape of the future.

I learned that those teenagers and others in Japan who were

staring at their mobile phones and twiddling the keyboards with their thumbs were sending words and simple graphics to each other—messages like short emails that were delivered instantly but could be read at any time. When I looked into the technical underpinnings of telephone texting, I found that those early texters were walking around with an always-on connection to the Internet in their hands. The tingling in my forebrain turned into a buzz. When you have a persistent connection to the Internet, you have access to a great deal more than a communication channel.

The Next Phase

A puzzling problem troubles those who understand the possibilities inherent in a mobile Internet: The potential power of connecting mobile devices to the Internet has been foreseen and hyped recently, but with the exception of DoCoMo, no company has yet created significant profits from wireless Internet services. The dotcom market collapse of 2001, accompanied by the even larger decline in value of global telecommunication companies, raised the question of whether any existing enterprises will have both the capital and the savvy to plug the Internet world into mobile telephony and make a successful business out of it.

Forecasting the technical potential of wireless Internet is the easy part. I knew that I should expect the unexpected when previously separate technologies meet. In the 1980s, television-like display screens plus miniaturized computers added up to a new technology with properties of its own: personal computers. PCs evolved dramatically over twenty years; today's handheld computer is thousands of times more powerful than the first Apple PC. Then PCs mated with telecommunications networks and multiplied in the 1990s to create the Internet, again spawning possibilities that neither of the parent technologies exhibited in isolation. Again, the new hybrid medium started evolving rapidly; my Internet connection today is thousands of times faster than my modem of the early 1980s. Then the Web in the late 1990s put a visual control panel on the Net and opened it to hundreds of millions of mainstream users. What's next in this self-accelerating spiral of technological, economic, and social change?

Next comes the mobile Net. Between 2000 and 2010, the social networking of mobile communications will join with the information-processing power of networked PCs. Critical mass will emerge some time after 2003, when more mobile devices than PCs will be connected to the Internet. If the transition period we are entering in the first decade of the twenty-first century resembles the advent of PCs and the Internet, the new technology regime will turn out to be an entirely new medium, not simply a means of receiving stock quotes or email on the train or surfing the Web while walking down the street. Mobile Internet, when it really arrives, will not be just a way to do things while moving. It will be a way to do things that couldn't be done before.

Better Hardware

Anybody who remembers what mobile telephones looked like five years ago has a sense of the pace at which handheld technology is evolving. Today's mobile devices are not only smaller and lighter than the earliest cell phones, they have become tiny multimedia Internet terminals. I returned to Tokyo a year and a half after I first noticed people using telephones to send text between tiny black and white screens. On my most recent visit in the fall of 2001, I conducted my own color videoconference conversations via the current version of high-speed, multimedia, "third-generation" mobile phones. Perhaps even more important than the evolution of color and video screens in telephone displays is the presence of "location awareness" in mobile telephones. Increasingly, handheld devices can detect, within a few yards, where they are located on a continent, within a neighborhood, or inside a room.

> *People might gain new powers at the same time we lose old freedoms.*

These separate upgrades in capabilities don't just add to each other; mobile, multimedia, location-sensitive characteristics multiply each other's usefulness. At the same time, their costs drop dramatically. . . . The driving factors of the mobile, context-sensitive, Internet-connected devices are Moore's Law (computer chips gets cheaper as they grow more powerful), Metcalfe's Law (the useful power of a network multiplies rapidly as the number of nodes in the network increases), and Reed's Law (the power of a network, especially one that enhances social networks, multiplies even more rapidly as the number of different human groups that can use the network increases). Moore's Law drove the PC industry and the cultural changes that resulted, Metcalfe's Law drove the deployment of the Internet, and Reed's Law will drive the growth of the mobile and pervasive Net.

The personal handheld device market is poised to take the kind of jump that the desktop PC made between 1980 and 1990, from a useful toy adopted by a subculture to a disruptive technology that changes every aspect of society. The hardware upgrades that make such a jump possible are already in the product pipeline. The underlying connective infrastructure is moving toward completion.

> *Mobile Internet, when it really arrives, will not be just a way to do old things while moving. It will be a way to do things that couldn't be done before.*

After a pause to recover from the collapse of the telecommunications economic bubble of the 1990s, the infrastructure for global, wireless, Internet-based communication is entering the final stages of development. The pocket videophone I borrowed in Tokyo was proof that a high-speed wireless network could link wireless devices and deliver multimedia to the palm of my hand. The most important next step for the companies that would deploy this technology and profit from it has nothing to do with chips or network protocols but everything to do with business models, early adopters, communities of developers, and value chains. It's not just about building the tools anymore. Now it's about what people use the tools to do.

A New Society

How will human behavior shift when the appliances we hold in our hands, carry in our pockets, or wear in our clothing become supercomputers that talk to each other through a wireless mega-Internet? What can we reasonably expect people to do when they get their hands on the new gadgets? Can anyone foresee which companies will drive change and detect which businesses will be transformed or rendered obsolete by it? These questions first occurred to me on that spring day in Tokyo, but I didn't think about it again until another sight on a street halfway around the world from Shibuya Crossing caught my attention.

> *The same convergence of technologies that opens new vistas of cooperation also makes possible a universal surveillance economy and empowers the bloodthirsty as well as the altruistic.*

Sitting at an outdoor café in Helsinki [Finland] a few months after I noticed the ways that people were using Japanese "i-mode" telephones, I watched five Finns meet and talk on the sidewalk. Three were in their early twenties. Two were old enough to be the younger people's parents. One of the younger persons looked down at his mobile phone while he was talking to one of the older people. The young man smiled and then showed the screen of his telephone to his peers, who looked at each other and smiled. However, the young man holding the device didn't show his mobile phone's screen to the older two. The sidewalk conversation among the five people flowed smoothly, apparently unperturbed by the activities I witnessed. Whatever the younger three were doing, it was clearly part of an accepted social code I knew nothing about. A new mode of social communication, enabled by a new technology, had already diffused into the norms of Finnish society. . . .

Early Signs of a Revolution

We're only seeing the first-order ripple effects of mobile-phone behavior now—the legions of the oblivious, blabbing into their hands or the air as they walk, drive, or sit in a concert and the electronic tethers that turn everywhere into the workplace and all the time into working time. What if these are just foreshocks of a future upheaval? I've learned enough from past technology shifts to expect the second-order effects of mobile telecommunications to bring a social tsunami. Consider a few of the early warning signs:

- The "People Power II" smart mobs in Manila [capital of the Philippines] who overthrew the presidency of President [Joseph] Estrada in 2001 organized demonstrations by forwarding text messages via cell phones.
- A Web site, http://www.upoc.com, enables fans to stalk their favorite celebrities in real time through Internet-organized mobile networks and provides similar channels for journalists to organize citizen-reporters on the fly. The site makes it easy for roving phone tribes to organize communities of interest.
- In Helsinki and Tokyo you can operate vending machines with your telephone and receive directions on your wireless organizer that show you how to get from where you are standing to where you want to go.
- "Lovegety" users in Japan find potential dates when their devices recognize another Lovegety in the vicinity broadcasting the appropriate pattern of attributes. Location-based matchmaking is now available on some mobile phone services.
- When I'm not using my computer, its processor searches for extraterrestrial intelligence. I'm one of millions of people around the world who lend their computers to a co-operative effort—distributing parts of problems through the Internet, running the programs on our PCs while the machines are idle, and assembling the results via the Net. These computation collectives produce enough supercomputing power to crack codes, design medicines, or render digital films.

Location-sensing wireless organizers, wireless networks, and community supercomputing collectives all have one thing in common: *They enable people to act together in new ways and in situations where collective action was not possible before.* An unanticipated convergence of technologies is suggesting new responses to civilization's founding question, How can competing individuals learn to work cooperatively?

Side Effects

As indicated by their name, smart mobs are not always beneficial. Lynch mobs and mobocracies continue to engender atrocities. The same convergence of technologies that opens new vistas of cooperation also makes possible a universal surveillance economy and empowers the bloodthirsty as well as the altruistic.

Like every previous leap in technological power, the new convergence of wireless computation and social communication will enable people to improve life and liberty in some ways and to degrade it in others. The same technology has the potential to be used as both a weapon of social control and a means of resistance. Even the beneficial effects will have side effects.

We are moving rapidly into a world in which the spying machinery is built into every object we encounter. Although we leave digital traces of our personal lives with our credit cards and Web browsers today, tomorrow's mobile devices will broadcast clouds of personal data to invisible monitors all around us as we move from place to place. We are living through the last years of the long era before sensors are built into the furniture. The scientific and economic underpinnings of pervasive computing have been building for decades, and the social side-effects are only beginning to erupt. The virtual, social, and physical worlds are colliding, merging, and coordinating.

Don't mistake my estimates of the power of the coming technology with unalloyed enthusiasm for its effects. I am not calling for an uncritical embrace of the new regime, but for an informed consideration of what we're getting ourselves into. We have an opportunity now to consider the social implications of this new technological regime as it first emerges, before every aspect of life is reordered.

> *Wireless devices will take reputation systems into every cranny of the social world.*

Online social networks are human activities that ride on technical communications infrastructures of wires and chips. When social communication via the Internet became widespread, people formed support groups and political coalitions online. The new social forms of the last decade of the twentieth century grew from the Internet's capability for many-to-many social communication. The new social forms of the early twenty-first-century will greatly enhance the power of social networks.

Since my visits to Tokyo and Helsinki, I've investigated the convergence of portable, pervasive, location-sensitive, intercommunicating devices with social practices that make the technologies useful to groups as well as individuals. Foremost among these social practices are the "reputation systems" that are beginning to spring up online—computer-mediated trust brokers. The power of smart mobs comes in part from the way age-old social practices surrounding trust and cooperation are being mediated by new communication and computation technologies.

A Matter of Trust

In this coming world, the acts of association and assembly, core rights of free societies, might change radically when each of us will be able to know who in our vicinity is likely to buy what we have to sell, sell what we want to buy, know what we need to know, want the kind of sexual or political encounter we also want. As online events are woven into the fabric of our physical world, governments and corporations will gain even more power over our behavior and beliefs than large institutions wield today. At the same time, citizens will discover new ways to band together to resist powerful institutions. A new kind of digital divide ten years from now will separate those who know how to use new media to band together from those who don't.

Knowing who to trust is going to become even more important. Banding together, from lynch mobs to democracies, taps the power of collective action. At the core of collective action is reputation—the histories each of us pull behind us that others routinely inspect to decide our value for everything from conversation partners to mortgage risks. Reputation systems have been fundamental to social life for a long time. In intimate societies, everyone knows everyone, and everyone's biography is an open, if not undisputed, book. Gossip keeps us up to date on who to trust, who other people trust, who is important, and who decides who is important.

Today's online reputation systems are computer-based technologies that make it possible to manipulate in new and powerful ways an old and essential human trait. Note the rise of Web sites like eBay (auctions), Epinions (consumer advice), Amazon (books, CDs, electronics), Slashdot (publishing and conversation) built around the contributions of millions of customers, enhanced by reputation systems that police the quality of the content and transactions exchanged through the sites. In each of these businesses, the consumers are also the producers of what they consume, the value of the market increases as more people use it, and the aggregate opinions of the users provide the measure of trust necessary for transactions and markets to flourish in cyberspace.

Reputation reports on eBay give prospective auction bidders a sense of the track record of the otherwise anonymous people to whom they may trustingly mail a check. Ratings of experts on Epinions make visible the experience of others in trusting each expert's advice. Moderators on Slashdot award "karma points" that make highly knowledgeable, amusing, or useful posts in an online conversation more visible than those considered less insightful.

Wireless devices will take reputation systems into every cranny of the social world, far from the desktops to which these systems are currently anchored. As the costs of communication, coordination, and social accounting services drop, these devices make possible new ways for people to self-organize mutual aid. It is now technologically possible, for example, to create a service that would enable you to say to your handheld device: "I'm on my way to the office. Who is on my route and is looking for a ride in my direction right now—and who among them is recommended by my most trusted friends?". . .

Dangers and Opportunities

Loss of privacy is perhaps the most obvious shadow side of technological cooperation systems. In order to cooperate with more people, I need to know more about them, and that means that they will know more about me. The tools that enable cooperation also transmit to a large number of others a constellation of intimate data about each of us. In the recent past, it was said that digital information technology, such as the magnetic strips on credit cards, leaves a "trail of electronic breadcrumbs" that can be used to track individuals. In the future, the trail will become a moving cloud as individuals broadcast information about themselves to devices within ten yards, a city block, or the entire world. Although there is room for speculation about how quickly the new tools will be adopted, certainly over the next several decades inexpensive wireless devices will penetrate into every part of the social world, bringing efficiencies to the production of snooping power. The surveillance state that [author George] Orwell feared was puny in its power in comparison to the panoptic web we have woven around us. Detailed information about the minute-by-minute behaviors of entire populations will become cost-effective and increasingly accurate. Both powerfully beneficial and powerfully dangerous potentials of this new tracking capability will be literally embedded in the environment.

Cooperative effort sounds nice, and at its best, it is the foundation of the finest creations of human civilizations, but it can also be nasty if the people who cooperate share pernicious goals. Terrorists and organized criminals have been malevolently successful in their use of smart mob tactics. A technological infrastructure that increases surveillance on citizens and empowers terrorists is hardly utopian. Intrusions on individual privacy and liberty by the state and its political enemies are not the only possible negative effects of enhanced technology-assisted cooperation. In addition, profound questions about the quality and meaning of life are raised by the prospect of millions of people possessing communication devices that are "always on" at home and work. How will mobile communications affect family and societal life?

There are opportunities as well as dangers, however; ... [I have a] growing belief that what we understand about the future of smart mobs, and how we talk about that future, holds the power to influence that future—at least within a short window of opportunity. The possibilities for the use of smart mob infrastructure do not consist exclusively of dark scenarios. Indeed, cooperation is integral to the highest expressions of human civilization. In counterpoint to the dystopian possibilities I've noted, I introduce sociologists and economists who argue that wireless technologies could make it easier to create public goods, thus affording an unprecedented opportunity for enhancing social capital that can enrich everyone's life.

Just as existing notions of community were challenged by the emergence of social networks in cyberspace, traditional ideas about the nature of place are being challenged as computing and communication devices begin to saturate the environment. As more people on city streets and on public transportation spend more time speaking to other people who are not physically co-present, the nature of public spaces and other aspects of social geography are changing before our eyes and ears; some of these changes will benefit the public good and others will erode it. . . .

I also know that beneficial uses of technologies will not automatically emerge just because people hope they will. Those who wish to have some influence on the outcome must first know what the dangers and opportunities are and how to act on them. Such knowledge does not guarantee that the new tools will be used to create a humane, sustainable world. Without such knowledge, however, we will be ill equipped to influence the world our grandchildren will inhabit.

3

The Internet Will Speed Up Human Evolution

Danny Belkin

Danny Belkin holds a PhD in immunology from Cambridge University. He works in the biotechnology field, and has written a number of articles on the future of the Internet.

The development of multicelled organisms came about as the result of cooperation between multiple single-celled organisms. Similarly, the Internet has enabled the cooperation between multiple single-brained organisms that, once technology has sufficiently advanced, will eventually merge into a conscious, multibrained collective mind made up of both human and computer components. The individual components of the collective will continue to exist as individuals, but their brains will also share the knowledge of the collective mind. Although many will choose not to participate in the collective mind, those who do will achieve an evolutionary step toward higher consciousness.

The discussion regarding the fate of the human race . . . has focused mainly on the question of technologies which might endanger that future. One specific threat which has been discussed is the danger posed to humans from a superior robot species. While the discussion itself is an important and relevant one, I would suggest that robotics and other technological developments may yet, should we avoid self-destruction, free us from worry about such threats, and instead present us with a future quite different from the common "humankind manages not to destroy itself and sets out to colonise the galaxy" scenario.

The drive for scientific and technological development during the last century, while indeed creating great dangers to our very existence, has brought us to the brink of a major change not only in the way we live, but in who we are—both individually and as a species. In this broad field of advanced technology, communications and information technology are unique in that they facilitate the advances in technology and push us toward the immense leap that we, as a species, are set to make.

A similar, if slightly less complex situation occurred on this planet a long time ago.

Multicellularity

Many millions of years ago, the first living cells evolved. These ancient unicellular organisms, swimming about in the primordial soup, had a sole function—survival in order to reproduce. Their chances of survival could be jeopardised by the conditions in which they lived, parasites, or other cells competing with them for the same energy source.

Over millions of years, the evolving cells acquired increasingly sophisticated ways to cope with these threats. They developed biological mechanisms that could counter the damaging effect of their surroundings, offensive mechanisms and defensive counter-measures to cope with the competing organisms and, ultimately, co-operation between cells of the same species.

> *The drive for scientific and technological development during the last century . . . has brought us to the brink of a major change . . . in who we are.*

Offensive mechanisms could be used by these cells in order to achieve superiority over competing organisms, allowing the triumphant cells to reproduce and proliferate. These mechanisms are believed to have been the precursors for the much more complex systems that control cell death in higher organisms. Cell death processes, tweaked and refined during evolution, entered a new stage upon the emergence of Eukaryotes. These more highly evolved cells contained cellular bodies and compartments, in which more complex biological processes occur.

Over the eons during which these cells evolved, communication and co-operation between individual cells emerged as key factors in the struggle for survival under adverse conditions. Over millions of years, this co-operation increased to the point at which the cells combined to become multicellular organisms.

An Evolutionary Leap

The emergence of multicellular organisms can be viewed as a highly significant leap forward in the evolutionary process. It was the first time individual organisms had established a permanent connection with one another in order to collectively enhance their chances of survival. These primitive multicellular organisms developed complex intra- and inter-cellular signaling networks, some of which were aimed at regulating cell death. These increased their chances of survival by getting rid of the cells least likely to cope with the environment and thus minimising energy expenditure by the organism. Dead cells could also be used to shield the multicellular organisms from the environment. Some of these mechanisms, such as the protective dead outer layers of the skin, are still evident in humans.

Thus, programmed cell death (PCD), generally defined as a biological mechanism for the removal of superfluous, infected, or damaged cells by activation of an intrinsic suicide program, gives a cell population the "ability" to select its fittest cells. It also allows a cell population to adapt its numbers to a changing environment.

These terms "selection", "adapt", "fit" are familiar to us from the theory of evolution. However, PCD and the theory of evolution may have more in common than mere terminology. PCD is a mechanism that is used extensively during an organism's development, mainly for optimising connections between cells and killing potentially harmful or redundant cells. Thus, it allows the killing of those cells that have grown incorrectly and/or have been damaged. In other words, harmless cells that have developed in the appropriate circumstances (in which the cell's microenvironment and neighboring cells supply the suitable conditions) will survive. In evolutionary terms, only the "fit" cells will survive. This "micro-evolution" during an organism's growth makes it possible for the individual to achieve the best functional interconnected cell population, based upon the genetic blueprint for that organism.

Altering Evolution

Homo sapiens and other highly evolved species have a long life span, and as a consequence the rate of their evolution is very slow. This is clearly evident in comparison with bacteria, which mutate rapidly and can therefore cope with adverse conditions that would otherwise wipe out an entire population. A rapid mutation rate can lead to the emergence of an individual whose genetic makeup has changed enough to allow it to grow even in an unfavorable environment. This rapid evolution is the underlying cause of the appearance of bacteria that are resistant to antibiotics. The slow pace of genetic mutation and selection in organisms higher on the evolutionary scale promoted the development of biological systems that would allow these organisms to cope with changes in the environment and attack by other living creatures in another way—not by genetic mutation and selection of the fittest organisms for survival, but by adaptation of the "selection" process into the organism, becoming a process that occurs within the organism during its lifetime.

> *Better means of communication allow the pooling of our knowledge[, which] . . . in turn fuels accelerated communication.*

In humans, this "selective" PCD process, especially during the development of the central nervous system (CNS), is one of the factors enabling the thinking process and intelligence. In the brain, the death of unnecessary cells means that only those cells with the best connections to their neighboring cells will survive, thus ensuring the optimal configuration and "wiring" of brain neurons. In illustrating this, researchers used a computer neural network model to examine the value of neuronal overproduction and the role of PCD in the development of the brain. They found that neuronal overproduction, with the subsequent deletion of neurons, allowed significantly greater learning ability (problem-solving ability) than that accomplished when starting out with only the necessary number of neurons. In more developed organisms PCD is an important factor in the creation of the networks, allowing complex brain functions.

Another important area in which PCD is utilized in humans

is the immune system. A vast number of potentially harmful pathogens are present in our environment. These micro-organisms possess rapid rates of mutation, which lead to the emergence of strains capable of surviving natural human defense mechanisms or modern antibiotics. Humans and other advanced organisms take longer to evolve, as their genetic changes occur during much longer time periods, and thus must develop a mechanism to cope with this constant attack. In response to this need, the immune system—in which massive killing of unnecessary and potentially harmful cells occurs during early development—was developed and grew progressively more complex during evolution.

Thus, the development of both the immune and the central nervous systems can be viewed as the result of a change in the evolutionary process of selection, from a process that occurs within a population and is influenced by the surrounding environment to an internal developmental process that supplies humans with intelligence and consciousness (through development of a complex brain) and the ability to fend off attack from pathogens (through a defensive immune system).

Carrying this line of thought further, it can be argued that the development of intelligence and consciousness has enabled humans to begin "disconnecting" from the classical evolutionary selection process. Developed countries offer their citizens modern medicine, which means that in most cases people now survive the bacterial and viral infections that would have killed them during the first half of the 20th century, and instead die from heart disease, cancer, neurodegenerative diseases, and other aging-related, inherent dysfunctions of the human body, for which cures will probably be found in the future.

> *The merging of humans into a super-high-bandwidth computer network will bring about the next level of human evolution: a human-computer meta-network.*

Furthermore, the way in which human genes are spread has changed. No longer are they transmitted according to the evolutionary maxim of "survival of the fittest." Modern norms and perceptions have a stronger effect on the process of mating than choosing the strongest male in the tribe. Most individuals marry only once or twice and consequently do not spread their genes widely. The genetically and physically "weak" do not die, and thus weak genetic traits are passed on and do not disappear. It thus seems that the way in which the process of evolution occurs has changed; it is no longer a process involving the selection of the fittest organisms, but has turned into a neuronal developmental one. Occurring in the brain, it allows us to overcome the mainly physical factors which used to play such an important part in determining which individuals would survive and which wouldn't; and it clearly influences the way genes are spread (geeks are now good prospects!).

Networked Humanity

Human culture and science advance by means of the pooling of information, whether acquired through meetings, correspondence, or literature. Thus, communication is the method by which human knowledge and technological ability continue to progress. Better means of communication allow the pooling of our knowledge in more efficient ways, giving rise to a more rapid pace of scientific and technological research and development. This in turn fuels accelerated communication, the result of which we can see today as an explosion in technological advancement.

> *The simplicity of information distribution . . . lies at the heart of the Internet. This sharing is set to develop as technology does, leading ultimately to a state in which information flows freely.*

What does this have to do with PCD and evolution? As proposed earlier, humanity has all but ceased to evolve in the way described by [biologist Charles] Darwin—by the incorporation and utilization of PCD as an evolutionary system, allowing intelligence (a process which occurred over millions of years). And intelligence itself, brought forth and refined by various mechanisms for the selection and connection of the fittest cells, has created the means to facilitate better communications between human beings. The latest step in this process is the Internet—which, to use a worn out cliché, "is bringing people closer together."

This advancement in interpersonal communications is set to continue, the ultimate stage being the development of a totally integrated system of human communication, which is likely to be achieved by highly advanced human-computer interface systems. Preliminary research on this subject is already being done, for example in the implantation of artificial retinas, connected to the optic nerve, into eyes of blind people. As computers are already interconnected, the merging of humans into a super-high-bandwidth computer network will bring about the next level of human evolution: a human-computer meta-network.

> *The development of communications technology has goals that transcend the immediate aim of, say, enabling people to surf the net using a cellular phone.*

Just as the merging of a large number of individual cells ultimately led to the development of consciousness, the merging of humans into an interconnected computer meta-network will eventually create a collective consciousness for all the individual participants. The forerunner of this "global" consciousness is already evident: our world is already described as a global village. Mass media, the Internet, and present-day communications make it possible for people with access to these services to know instantly what is going on in every part of the globe. Information is much more immediately accessible; withholding it from the public much more difficult. As a consequence, public opinion (stemming from the emerging global consciousness) has become such an important factor that the media has become a major fighting ground for governments.

The way in which information technology is progressing shows that we are already quite far along this road. The simplicity of information distribution, be it sharing of music, ideas, or any other data, lies at the heart of the Internet. This sharing is set to develop as technology does, leading ultimately to a state in which information flows freely.

Computing power sharing on the Internet is another area

that demonstrates the power of the network, and its importance is likely to increase. . . . Up to now, most computers have been used as end-terminals for information accessed through the net. The true capabilities and potential of an interconnected computer network, even in terms of raw processing power, are mind-boggling. Imagine what a network of fully interconnected humans, their mental abilities pooled and enhanced, will be like.

Questions and Thoughts

To the majority of observers, the development of modern technology must seem as a random, uncontrolled process. Metaphorically, we are seen as riding out of control on this mustang called technological development. The individuals who make this happen are motivated by various forces: some are in it for the money, some for the pure fascination of scientific discovery, and some want to make the world a better place. Consider, as an example, the currently booming technology of [information technology]. The development of communications technology has goals that transcend the immediate aim of, say, enabling people to surf the net using a cellular phone. There is a tendency to look only at the immediate, everyday-life implications of this technology, rather than seeing what lies at the end of the path we are taking. Increasing the bandwidth more and more, pulling individuals closer and closer together, are steps in a process that will ultimately lead to the unification of the human race.

The high capacity of data transfer and high level of communications between individuals is the key to development of a unified total consciousness. Physically, though, individuals are likely to remain separate. This is a an important point, as even though the interconnected masses will operate for the advancement of the whole, a degree of individuality and autonomy, as the individual cells in our body possess, is vital. Furthermore, the flow of data between individuals will not be entirely unobstructed, as the single mind will not be able to cope with such vast amounts of information. Certain filters will have to be set up and maintained to sort out the relevant from the irrelevant data.

At some point after the integration of humans and machines, an additional step will have to be taken: incorporation of PCD, resulting in disconnection of the weaker links (or individual constituents) from the collective network. Only once

PCD, or the principle underlying it, has been incorporated will it be possible to accomplish the leap to a higher state of consciousness and intelligence—an intelligence which is the sum of all the minds connected to the network, and which lies beyond what any of us can imagine.

> **❝** *Why would anyone voluntarily relinquish control of an independent consciousness, allowing personal thoughts, memories and consciousness to be shared, at a certain level, by the entire population?* **❞**

A related aspect concerns loss of privacy. Will people want this to happen at all? Why would anyone voluntarily relinquish control of an independent consciousness, allowing personal thoughts, memories and consciousness to be shared, at a certain level, by the entire population? The answer, which may sound frightening, is that the obvious choice will be between acceptance of one's integration into the network and consequent loss of individualism through joining the superorganism, or remaining separate, outside it. Those not joining will sentence themselves to being the lesser life forms of this planet, lower on the evolutionary scale. Ponder for one moment the difference between a human and a bacterium.

Inevitable Progress

The pooling of human consciousness may begin with the transferral of all our knowledge to computers. This is already happening on the Internet. At a later stage of scientific advancement, a physical connection of humans to the matrix at higher and higher levels (via advances in nervous/computer interface technology) will be possible. Thereafter, with humans completely interconnected through a network, questions might arise as to the relevance of the physical world. Could we simply upload all our consciousness to this virtual world? Would we then create a comparable world inside the network?

As mentioned earlier, the creation of multicellular organisms can be viewed as an evolutionary leap. The same might be said about the integration of human and machine to create a wholly interconnected "organism", composed of multitudes of individuals. It will be an immense leap for humanity, or for what it becomes. This idea has been put forward by scientists and by writers of science fiction. It may be seen as good ("enlightenment through computers") or bad . . . —the end of humanity as we know it, a utopia, or both.

It seems, though, that this is not an appropriate question: humanity will have to come to terms with the fact that it is but an insignificant part of the universe, and as such must conform to its physical and biological laws and their resulting processes, among them evolution. Whether we like it or not, the time has come when our evolution has brought us to a doorway, beyond which lies what we cannot grasp by means of our limited, single-brain-power thought. We cannot possibly fathom the thoughts and conscious scope of billions of linked minds, acting together.

This vision may seem horrifying to some, thrilling to others. It is the next major evolutionary step forward for humanity, and will eventually be taken. However we choose to view this scenario, the fact remains that this is the future toward which we are inevitably heading.

This is not about good or bad. It is about evolution. Humankind must evolve.

4

Internet Voting Will Improve the Democratic Process

Justin Matlick

Justin Matlick is a former senior fellow in information studies at the Pacific Research Institute, a public policy think tank.

One way to restore confidence in U.S. elections and encourage more young Americans to vote is to establish a more convenient and less ambiguous voting method based on electronics rather than paper ballots. Although some legitimate concerns regarding possible fraud, security lapses, and unequal access exist, most could be addressed over time using a two-part phase-in process. During the first phase, electronic voting machines would be available at every voting station. Election officials could then apply lessons learned during that phase to a second phase, in which home Internet voting would also be permitted.

In the [2000] election's aftermath,[1] the search for a better voting system is on. Despite potential flaws, Internet voting will eventually prove to be the best way to ensure the accuracy and fairness of elections. To restore public faith in American democracy, Congress should start phasing in an online system now.

1. During the 2000 presidential election, problems with ballots in Florida resulted in a partial hand-counting. George W. Bush won the election despite Al Gore winning the popular vote. Critics partly blamed the Florida ballot counting problem for the election results.

Today's vote-tabulation systems simply cannot be trusted to decide close elections. This fact, now widely understood, has made a disinterested electorate even more cynical. To prevent a further decline in voter turnout, the margin of error in federal elections must be substantially reduced by a new mechanism the public trusts.

> **❝❝ To restore public faith in American democracy, Congress should start phasing in an online system now. ❞❞**

Existing Internet voting systems, which are simple and straightforward, could accomplish this goal. Using computers stationed at home, work, or in polling places, voters log on using a personal identification number. They then click on markers denoting their candidate of choice. Finally, the system asks them to verify their ballot before forwarding it to central computers. Tabulation, freed from paper ballots and vote-counting machines, is automatic, accurate, and fair.

Recent tests have revealed another benefit: increased voter participation. For example, when Arizona used online voting in its [2000] Democratic primary, turnout more than doubled. Participation was particularly high among technology-savvy 18–34 year olds, who usually keep silent on Election Day.

Challenges Posed by Online Voting

Despite this benefit, critics accurately point out that Internet systems face several hurdles. Fraud and security are the biggest concerns. Without face-to-face contact, it remains difficult to verify voters' identities: theoretically, a single person could buy up and cast large numbers of votes.

Hackers pose a more troubling threat. According to California's Internet Voting Task Force, insecure computers could be secretly infected with election-altering viruses. These programs could automatically change and transmit individual ballots without the voter's knowledge. Online voting could also be hampered by civic concerns.

Internet-driven participation increases could negatively affect the demographics of the voting populations. Minorities and the poor are far less likely to have Internet access. As the Virginia-based Voting Integrity Project has argued, Internet voting could, therefore, give an unfair advantage to affluent citizens; higher turnout by wealthier voters could dilute the importance of minority votes.

These problems, however, can be solved over time. Digital signature technology could be employed to verify identities. Internet security systems already safeguard trillions of dollars in financial transactions, and similar structures can be designed to protect votes. The digital divide is shrinking rapidly. . . .

A Two-Stage Process

Since the common denominator among these problems is distance, the logical solution is to employ an incremental approach that initially eliminates this factor. Federal legislators should act now to promote such an approach. Though Congress cannot impose uniform voting standards, it can—and should—quickly declare support for online voting, give states incentives to establish the necessary technological infrastructure, and provide suggested implementation guidelines. These should be centered around a two-step process.

Phase one would replace ballot boxes with computer terminals, but limit Internet voting to official polling places. This would circumvent the distance-related problems, ensuring safety and equity by limiting voting to official, secure computers. It also would allow the public to become familiar with the new process. . . .

The goal of phase two would be unlimited Internet voting. . . . Even the most conservative estimates suggest that Internet access will be nearly ubiquitous [within] eight years. . . .

If Congress follows this plan, it can begin leading America out of its post election quagmire. Internet voting would ensure higher levels of accuracy and fairness. By tapping into the current technology-based optimism, it would help reinvigorate public confidence in American democracy. And it could ultimately facilitate a more active voting public this country sorely needs. Failure to capitalize on this opportunity would not only contribute to the public's cynicism. It would justify it.

5

Internet Voting Would Harm the Democratic Process

John C. Dvorak

John C. Dvorak has been a regular columnist for PC Maga-zine *since 1986 and has written for numerous other com-puter publications as well; in total, he has written or cowrit-ten fourteen books and over four thousand published articles. He is also former host of the TechTV television series* Silicon Spin *and the National Public Radio series* Real Computing.

Those who support online voting tend to do so with very little knowledge of the potential problems involved in such a procedure. Online voting would be dangerous for four reasons. First, online voting is vulnerable to hackers. Second, because those voting online would do so unsupervised, they could be subject to threats or co-ercion. Third, poor citizens are less likely than rich citi-zens to have Internet access, which would create a seg-regated voting system. Finally, most citizens are not computer-literate; this increases the likelihood of voting errors. Moreover, although some say that online voting would be less expensive than traditional voting, there has been no evidence to support this assertion.

Despite its serious flaws, online voting is a topic that just re-fuses to die. The reasons vary but seem centered on two beliefs. One is that the [2000] election would have "gone the

John C. Dvorak, "Why Voting over the Internet Is Still a Really Bad Idea," *Com-puter Shopper*, vol. 24, May 2004, p. 42. Copyright © 2004 by CNET Networks, Inc. All rights reserved. Reproduced by permission.

other way" if just a few more people voted.[1] The other is that more than half the public actually wants to vote.

The debate never ends, and, each time, the idea is shot down for one reason or another. The most critical is the fact that various government and private studies indicate the Internet is not secure enough for any of this; hackers could hijack an election. With each new virus/Trojan/worm attack, we witness an increasing ferocity. Microsoft and others may talk a big game when it comes to security, but the fact remains: The computer medium is one of the most insecure imaginable, and experts who examine it closely all agree it cannot be made secure.

The Possibility of Corruption

With this in mind, you have to wonder about the motives of those promoting online voting. When I was in grammar school, we heard stories about how the evil Southern white Democrats would pay blacks to vote a certain way, then escort them into the voting booth, or simply vote in their place. Often they'd just keep them from voting. The stories were many and varied, but corruption was the theme.

The entire voting mechanism is still pretty delicate, and Florida's hanging-chad scandal is proof. Online voting will only encourage fraud and corruption. Is it inconceivable a less-than-ethical candidate might bribe a hacker to crack the system?

> *Is it inconceivable [that] a less-than-ethical candidate might bribe a hacker to crack the system?*

Even if the security infrastructure were flawless, exactly how would online voting ever work right? You could have a gun to someone's head as they voted, and nobody would know. And exactly how does online voting deal with the so-called digital divide? I'm envisioning voting parties where those without

1. During the 2000 presidential election, ballot counting machines in Florida malfunctioned and the ballots had to be counted by hand. The Supreme Court eventually called a halt to the hand count, and George W. Bush won over Al Gore, despite the fact that Gore had won the popular vote.

computers would go to a house, church, or school, and end up being strong-armed into voting for the collective choice, while people looked over their shoulders at every turn.

> **You could have a gun to someone's head as they voted, and nobody would know.**

About a decade ago, after expressing my doubts about the viability of online voting, I was inundated with mail from readers telling me how wrong I was and that online voting would be the future of democracy. I found this distressing, but I figured as the Internet's lackluster security became more apparent, and as people saw that high-school kids could crack "uncrackable" schemes, that thinking would change. If that didn't do it, then word of corruption within the system, backdoors [vulnerabilities] into software code, and a million other sneaky tricks would surely end this thinking once and for all.

Apparently, it was enough to make the Department of Defense [DOD] think twice. It canceled its Secure Electronic Registration and Voting Experiment (SERVE) for military and civilian citizens overseas, and there are currently no plans to allow online voting in [national] elections. The DOD made the decision after a panel of experts deemed the security of the Internet flawed and too irresistible a target for hackers. I found it amusing that promoters initially explained how it emulated the look and feel of the new computerized voting machines, as if this were a good thing.

The Advantages of Paper Ballots

Much of this modernization stems from some weird belief that easily audited paper ballots are suddenly no longer viable, even though they've worked well for more than 100 years. The newer systems will somehow save money and make the election go faster. They're better. New technology is always better, right?

I'm not convinced the money-saving assertions actually work. Salesmen can do miracles with numbers. As for the speed issue, what's the rush? It's not as if elections are taking place every week. This is a once-in-a-while exercise, and you want to do it right, not fast.

Those who think online voting is a good idea are clueless about computer and networking technologies. And those who sincerely believe it can be done safely and without incident are clueless about human behavior.

And let's not forget the people who would be doing the voting in the first place. Nearly 75 percent of respondents to a recent study conducted in England "did not care" whether an attachment was a virus. They clearly did not understand what the problem was. The fact is, people are generally not savvy about the computer technologies we take for granted. This reflects the electorate. They work best with paper and pencil. Let's keep it that way.

6

Education Will Not Move Online

David F. Noble

David F. Noble is professor of social sciences at York University and cofounder of the National Coalition for Universities in the Public Interest. He is also the author of twelve books, including Digital Diploma Mills: The Automation of Higher Education, *from which this viewpoint is taken.*

Online education emerged due primarily to two factors: enthusiasm about new technology, and simple greed. Collaboration between universities and for-profit information technology companies led to new, well-promoted online education initiatives, which briefly created the impression that online education would emerge as a replacement for on-campus instruction. Instead, the abject failure of these programs—combined with student and faculty protests against them—demonstrates that the dominance of online education is no longer inevitable. Online education is inferior to traditional classroom instruction for several reasons: It makes a personal mentor-student relationship impossible, it does not adequately protect the rights of faculty members, and it reduces the educational process to a consumer good, pre-packaged for mass consumption.

Far sooner than most observers might have imagined, the juggernaut of online education [has] appeared to stall. For the first few years after the pioneering initiatives to take higher education online were announced, it seemed there was no stop-

David F. Noble, *Digital Diploma Mills: The Automation of Higher Education.* New York: Monthly Review Press, 2001. Copyright © 2001 by the Monthly Review Foundation. Reproduced by permission.

ping it. Promoters of instructional technology and "distance learning" advanced with ideological bravado as well as institutional power, the momentum of human progress allegedly behind them. They had merely to proclaim "it's the future" to throw skeptics on the defensive and convince seasoned educators that they belonged in the dustbin of history. The monotonal mantras about our inevitable wired destiny, the prepackaged palaver of silicon snake-oil salesmen, echoed through the halls of academe, replete with sophomoric allusions to historical precedent (the invention of writing and the printing press) and sound bites about the imminent demise of the "sage on the stage" and "bricks and mortar" institutions. Only a year or two later, however, the wind was out of their sails, their momentum broken, their confidence shaken.

At countless campus forums on the subject throughout North America, the burden of proof was shifting from the critics to the promoters. Though still amply funded and politically supported, they had increasingly been put on the defensive. This is not to say that the pressures behind the online university had abated but that, ideologically at least, the terrain had changed irreversibly. By the end of 1998 promoters of the online university were compelled to try to buttress their still lame arguments with half-baked data about pedagogical usefulness, economic return, or market demand. Attendance at campus events multiplied by an order of magnitude as faculty and students finally became alert to the administrative agendas and commercial con games behind this seeming technological revolution.

> *The monotonal mantras about our inevitable wired destiny . . . echoed through the halls of academe. . . . Only a year or two later, however, the wind was out of their sails.*

Off campus, the scene was much the same. Study after study seemed to confirm that computer-based instruction reduces performance levels and that habitual Internet use induces depression. Advertisers were peddling platinum MasterCards and even Apple laptop computers by subtly acknowledging that "seven days without e-mail" is "priceless" and that being in touch with your office from anywhere anytime is a "bummer." Meanwhile, all the busy people supposedly clamoring for distance learning—who allegedly constitute the multibillion-dollar market for cyberinstruction—are curling up at night with *Tuesdays with Morrie*, a sentimental evocation of the intimate, enduring, and life-enriching relationship between a former student and his dying professor, [which spent] four years on the *New York Times* bestseller list. "Have you ever really had a teacher? One who saw you as a raw but precious thing, a jewel that, with wisdom, could be polished to a proud shine? If you are lucky enough to find such teachers, you will always find your way back." So much for distance learning.

Resisting Online Education

Above all, a specter came to haunt the high-tech hijackers of higher education, the specter of faculty (and student) resistance. . . .

At UCLA [the University of California at Los Angeles], the widely touted Instructional Enhancement Initiative, which mandated websites for all 3800 arts and sciences courses, floundered in the face of faculty recalcitrance and resistance. By the end of the first academic year, only 30 percent of the faculty had put any of their course material online and several dozen had actively resisted the initiative and the way it had been unilaterally inspired and implemented. UCLA Extension's partnership with the Home Education Network (which changed its name . . . to Onlinelearning.net) ran aground on similar shoals when instructors made it clear that they would refuse to assign any of their rights in their course materials to either UCLA (the Regents) or the company. In already up to their necks, the partners decided simply to claim the rights anyway and proceed apace, flying without wings on borrowed time.

The strike at York [University] awakened the faculty there to a new vigilance and militancy with regard to the computer-based commercialization of the university. It also emboldened others elsewhere. At Acadia University, for example, which had linked up with IBM in hopes of becoming the foremost wired institution in Canada, the threat of a faculty strike forced the administration to back off from some of their unilateral demands for online instruction, and faculties at other Canadian institutions have been moving in the same direction. Even within Simon Fraser University's Department of Communications, home of the recently refunded Canadian flagship Telelearning Research Center, serious faculty challenges to the virtual university enterprise have emerged and gone public.

In the United States as well, resistance was on the rise. Faculty and students in the California State University [CSU] system, the largest public higher educational institution in the country, fought vigorously and effectively against the California Educational Technology Initiative (CETI), an unprecedented deal between CSU and a consortium of firms (Microsoft, GTE, Hughes, and Fujitsu), which would have given them a monopoly over the development of the system's telecommunications infrastructure and the marketing and delivery of CSU online courses. Students resisted being made a captive market for company products while faculty responded to the lack of faculty consultation and threats to academic freedom and their intellectual property rights. In particular, they feared that CETI might try to dictate online course content for commercial advantage and that CSU would appropriate and commercially exploit their course materials.

> **In the California State University system . . . students resisted being made a captive market for [high tech] products.**

Throughout the CSU system, faculty senates passed resolutions against CETI, tried to obtain an injunction to stop the deal, and used the media and public forums to campaign against it. Together with students, faculty participated in widely publicized demonstrations; at Humboldt State University in northern California, students demonstrating against the deal altered the sign at the campus entrance to read "Microsoft University," a creative act of defiance which caught the attention of media around the country). Through the efforts of the Internet activist group NetAction, the controversy over the CETI deal became a cause célèbre, galvanizing opposition and leading to high-profile government hearings and legislative scrutiny and skepticism. Opposition to the deal from California-based business competitors such as Apple, Netscape, and Sun (none of the CETI partners were California-based) also contributed to the erosion of legislative support. (The deal may also have been unconstitutional under state law.) Before long, Microsoft and

Hughes dropped out, then GTE, and the deal was dead. Any new deal would be sure to encounter determined and well-organized opposition.

Further north at the University of Washington in Seattle, a campus with little recent history of faculty activism, four hundred faculty members attended a February 1998 forum on "digital diploma mills" sponsored by the local chapter of the AAUP [American Association of University Professors]. Later that spring, Washington governor Gary Locke and Wallace Loh, his chief advisor on higher education, gave speeches extolling the virtues of the "brave new world of digital education" and outlined plans for statewide initiatives in that direction. The AAUP immediately drafted an open letter to the governor vigorously opposing this vapid vision and circulated it among the faculty. Within two days, seven hundred faculty from across the campus, from Slavic studies to computer science, had signed the letter. Another two hundred signatures were later added and the letter was made public in early June. Within a week, this bold and eloquent faculty protest had made headlines around the country.

"We feel called upon to respond before quixotic ideas harden into disastrous policies," the faculty wrote the governor. "While costly fantasies of this kind present a mouth-watering bonanza to software manufacturers and other corporate sponsors, what they bode for education is nothing short of disastrous. . . . Education is not reducible to the downloading of information, much less to the passive and solitary activity of staring at a screen. Education is an intersubjective and social process, involving hands-on activity, spontaneity, and the communal experience of sharing in the learning enterprise. . . . We urge you to support learning as a human and social practice, an enrichment of soul and mind, the entitlement of all citizens in a democracy, and not a profit-making commodity to be offered on the cheapest terms to the highest bidder. The University of Washington is a vital resource to our community, not a factory, not a corporation, not a software package. Its excellence and integrity are not only assets that we as a community can afford to maintain, but also assets that we cannot afford to squander.". . .

The Backlash

The faculty actions at CSU [and] the University of Washington . . . were not isolated events. The ferment throughout academia became apparent at the international Digital Diploma Mills conference held at Harvey Mudd College in Claremont, California, in April 1998. The conference attracted well-informed faculty and student participants and an audience of campus activists and rank-and-file union members from throughout the United States and Canada, as well as Mexico. (The keynote speaker was Mary Burgan, general secretary of the AAUP, who suggested that "distance makes the heart grow colder.") The two days of sessions critically examined the political economy, pedagogical value, and economic viability of online education and explored the implications for faculty and students, while those in attendance used their free time to compare notes, make contacts, and extend their networks. The *Chronicle of Higher Education* ran a two-page story on the conference, which ended on a revealing note, pointing out that "officials at Harvey Mudd took pains to distance themselves from the event."

> *Education is not reducible to the downloading of information.*

At the same time, faculty and student activists have been holding similar forums on their own campuses. I myself have participated in many such events at campuses including the University of Pittsburgh, Alma College, James Madison University, Embry-Riddle University, George Mason University, the University of Western Ontario, the University of Wisconsin, the University of Washington, the California State University campuses in Sacramento and San Bernardino, California Polytechnic University in Pomona, and the University of California campuses at Irvine and Los Angeles. At all of these events it has become clear that faculty and students alike were realizing that this was a moment of reckoning, a "high noon" for higher education. They were overcoming their traditional timidity and parochialism to make common cause with like-minded people across the continent, to fight for their own and the larger public interest against the plans and pronouncements of peddlers and politicians who in general know little about education. Having learned that they are not alone, faculty found new confidence in their own experience and expertise, and in their rightful capacity to decide what is a good education. Socrates, they reminded themselves, was not a content provider.

In the wake of this resistance, the media caught the scent, publicly validating and magnifying its message. After several years of puff pieces and press releases about the wonders of wired learning, the media began to give the matter more scrutiny and critics their due. "Virtual Classes Trend Alarms Professors," the *New York Times* reported in June 1998; a front page article in the *Wall Street Journal* in August carried the headline "Scholarly Dismay: College Professors Balk at Internet Teaching Plans"; describing what it called the "backlash against virtual education," the *Christian Science Monitor* carried another summer story entitled "Professors Peer Doubtfully into a Digital Future"; the *Industry Standard*, "The Newsmagazine of the Internet Economy," began its feature article "Academics Rebel Against an Online Future" with the words: "Hell no—we won't go—online. . . . The backlash has begun."

The *San Francisco Chronicle*, the *Seattle Times*, the *Los Angeles Times*, the *Boston Globe*—all ran critical articles examining the commodification and commercialization of university instruction. In June 1998 the *Industry Standard's* cover story was "Ideas for Sale: Business is racing to bring education online. Now academics fear they're becoming just another class of content provider." The headline for the article read "Higher Earning: The Fight to Control the Academy's Intellectual Capital." In response to the open letter to the governor from University of Washington faculty that same month, the *Seattle Times* ran an editorial entitled "Potential Pitfalls," noting that "Signs of high tech corporate corruption are already sneaking into higher education classrooms." Indeed.

Failing Business Models

If the media-anointed "backlash" against virtual education has prompted a bit more skepticism on the part of reporters and editorial writers, so too has the pitiful performance of the virtuosi themselves, whose market appears to have been a mirage. After several years of high-profile hype and millions of dollars, the flagship Western Governors' Virtual University opened for business this fall [2001], offering hundreds of online courses. Expecting an initial enrollment of 5000, the WGU enrolled only 10 people, and received just 75 inquiries. Intended to put a positive spin on this disaster, WGU marketing director Jeff Edward's double-talk unwittingly hit the nail on the head: "it points out that students are pretty serious about this." Serious enough, that is, to know crap when they see it.

It was much the same story at Onlinelearning.net, the UCLA partner that described itself as "one of the leading global suppliers of online continuing education." The company lost two million dollars in its first year of business and was unable to pay UCLA the anticipated royalties. According to insiders, it was then losing about $60,000 a month. John Kobara, the president of the company and former UCLA vice chancellor for marketing, acknowledged at a company event in November 1998 that it was indeed a very risky business. Kobara noted that most apparent successes are misleading: at the universities of Colorado, Washington, and Arizona the great majority of alleged "distance-learning" customers "are in the dorms" while most online programs, such as those at Berkeley and Vanderbilt, have retention rates of well less than 50 percent. "Retention is the challenge," Kobara explained. Getting people enrolled is one thing, and difficult enough. Getting them to remain enrolled and complete their courses is another thing entirely. The New York Times of November 2 [2001] confirmed that these were not isolated experiences in an article entitled "More Colleges Plunging Into Uncharted Waters of On-Line Courses."

Socrates, [faculty] reminded themselves, was not a content provider.

Distance-learning administrators kept their chins up and issued upbeat press releases that became increasingly hard to believe. Officials at WGU, the Southern Regional Electronic Campus (SREC), which coordinates distance learning courses in sixteen southern states, and the California Virtual University [CVU], which coordinates the online offerings of one hundred California campuses, all expressed optimism about the future of distance learning. "We feel confident that there is tremendous interest, especially in the non-traditional student environment," said WGU's Jeffrey Xouris. "Figures indicate significant interest in distance education," said CVU's Rich Halberg. "The dirty little secret," Gerald Heeger, dean of Continuing and Professional Studies at NYU, told the New York Times, "is that nobody's making any money."

In each case the basic story was the same: great expectations have yielded great expenditures. The high-tech hallucinations of new revenue streams that so enchanted administrators everywhere were conjured up by voodoo demographics, which mistook distance for demand. What was left out of the equation was whether or not people, on the basis of convenience and computer gimmickry, would be willing to pay more for less education.

> **Distance-learning administrators kept their chins up and issued upbeat press releases that became increasingly hard to believe.**

In time-honored fashion, the purveyors of this dismal product turned to the taxpayer to bail them out. They placed their bets on the Distance Education Demonstration Program contained in the education bill approved by Congress and signed by [President] Bill Clinton in late 1998. This bill waives classroom requirements for federal student aid eligibility for distance learning customers, thereby priming the distance education market and providing an indirect subsidy to vendors. According to existing law, students had to spend a specified number of hours in a classroom to be eligible for student aid. Vendors had been lobbying for some time, against strenuous opposition from traditional academic institutions and unions, for a waiver of such requirements, which would render their customers eligible for student aid and them eligible for a handsome handout.

The new legislation granted such a waiver for fifteen organizations engaged exclusively in distance learning, including the Western Governors' University. But, even fattened with such pork, it was by no means assured that the distance-learning market would materialize on anything like the scale dreamed up by the wishful thinkers of Wall Street. An inflated assessment of the market for online distance education was matched by an abandonment of financial common sense, as officials recklessly allocated millions of (typically taxpayer) dollars toward untested virtual ventures. Suckered by the siren songs and scare tactics of the silicon snake-oil salesmen, university and college officials have thrown caution to the wind and failed to full-cost their pet projects. Former chief university financial officer Christopher Oberg warned at the Harvey Mudd conference that administrators had suspended normal accounting practices at their peril. (Little wonder that the presumably more sober Certified Public Accounts Review program at Northern Illinois University broke off its partnership with online vendor Real Education, citing questionable business practices.)

Quickly Obsolete

In the face of faculty and student resistance, increasing media skepticism, and notably lackluster performance, some university administrators began to break ranks. It is perhaps no surprise to hear a note of caution emanating from an elite private institution, which must retain some semblance of genuine education for its privileged clientele even while competing for their favors with high-wire acts. Yet it is nevertheless remarkable to find it coming from one of the nation's premier technical institutions, which famously foisted all of this technology upon us in the first place. Last year [2000] Michael Dertouzos, director of MIT's [Massachusetts Institute of Technology's] Laboratory for Computer Science—home of the World Wide Web—waxed eloquent about the virtues of non-virtual education. "Education is much more than the transfer of knowledge from teachers to learners. As an educator myself, I can say firsthand that lighting the fire of learning in the hearts of students, providing role models, and building student-teacher bonds are the most critical factors for successful learning. These cardinal necessities will not be imparted by information technology. . . . [T]eachers' dedication and ability will still be the most important educational tool." And now, Dertouzos's boss, MIT president Charles Vest, has added his voice to the chorus. "Even though I'm from MIT, I'm not convinced technology is the answer to everything." Vest conceded. In particular, the relationship between teacher and student "is an experience you can never replace electronically." Echoes of *Tuesdays with Morrie.*

More striking still was the inaugural address of J. Bernard Machen as president of the University of Utah. The University of Utah is located in Salt Lake City, the headquarters of the WGU, and among the distinguished guests at the inauguration was Utah governor and WGU co-chairman Michael Leavitt, who once proclaimed that "in the future an institution of higher education will become a little like a local television station." Formerly the provost at the University of Michigan, Machen forcefully decried the vocational emphasis on online learning and the shifting allocation of public higher education resources toward virtual instruction at the expense of traditional campus-based education. "Let us not succumb to the temptation to force a college education to its lowest common denominator," Machen insisted. "It inherently limits the broader, more interactive aspects of a university education. Spontaneous debate, discussion, and exchange of ideas in the classroom are essential in developing the mind. Poetry must be heard, interpreted and discussed, with professors and classmates. Learning about the different professions and academic disciplines available at the University of Utah requires personal involvement, and that is only available on our campus, and it can only be experienced by being here. . . . The kind of education I am describing is not the cheapest, but it is the best."

Predictably, Machen's remarks were derisively dismissed by Governor Leavitt's office. "It is not the first time that we have heard a kind of fearful, skeptical reaction of the higher education community," one aide to the governor remarked, in a condescending manner all too familiar to faculty critics. But they were not listening carefully, for this is not what they had heard before. No longer were students and faculty (and the rare administrator) speaking up for quality education out of fear and defensiveness in the face of a preordained and prematurely foreclosed virtual future. Emboldened by recent experience (and forewarned by the disastrous demise of public health care), their voices now took on new-found conviction and resolve. The tide had turned. Indeed, it is now the tired response of the governor's office that appears time-worn and out of touch, the damning words strangely hollow without the weight of history behind them. The bloom is off the rose.

7

Internet Dating Will Lead to the Commodification of People

Heather Havrilesky

Heather Havrilesky is a freelance writer and cartoonist, and a regular contributor to National Public Radio's radio program All Things Considered.

Internet dating sites offer those who use them an almost unlimited range of dating options, but this comes with a cost. Dating profiles are necessarily written and designed to attract others, so they're created essentially as advertisements. Those the profiles are meant to attract are dealt with as customers. In order to compete for customers, users create increasingly appealing advertisements for themselves—advertisements that become more difficult to resist, but virtually impossible to live up to. The result is that when young men and women meet actual people—not the online personas posted on dating Web sites—they are inevitably disappointed because these people are not perfect.

The golden age of online dating is upon us. Just ask executives of Match.com, who last month [June 2002] reported a 195 percent increase in paid subscribers over the same quarter last year. Or look at Yahoo, where online personals have increased the company's revenues despite a decline in income

Heather Havrilesky, "Meatmarket.com," Salon.com, May 15, 2002. This article first appeared in Salon.com, at www.Salon.com. An online version remains in the Salon archives. Reprinted with permission.

from advertising. Or talk to any youngish single person in New York. When I asked a friend, who met her last boyfriend online, how many of her single friends had used or are currently using online dating services, she replied, "Pretty much all of them."

Look no further than the "Personals of the Day" you see pop up on this site [Salon.com], as well as *The Onion* and countless other sites, and you'll realize two things: One, online personals have become a major source of revenue for content sites, and two, there are some damn fine-looking young folks floating around out there. Unless Spring Street Networks, the source of those ads, has been inventing fictional singles with a crack team of models, stylists, marketers and professional photographers, there appear to be a great many attractive people online these days, shamelessly hamming it up in the hopes of meeting that special anyone.

It's a far cry from the spring of 1996, when I attended a party for Match.com that was populated primarily by computer programmers who looked like they hadn't left the server room of their start-up offices in several months, their only contact with other humans limited to those moments when they braved the weak San Francisco sunlight to fetch a banana moon pie from the company's vending machine, or to scuttle over to Cafe Centro for a quadruple nonfat latte. That tall blond girl who worked there sure was cute, but she was sort of mean!

> **❝***Why have people begun peddling themselves so shamelessly online?***❞**

Now that blond girl is prominently featured on the pages of Match.com, pensively biting a manicured finger while lounging across an unmade bed in her nightie under the moniker "sweet 'n' dirty."

So how did everything change so quickly, and why have people begun peddling themselves so shamelessly online?

The truth is, most young people see nothing the least bit embarrassing about online dating or "man shopping" as one woman referred to it in a recent *New York Times* article. Maybe kids today are far less self-conscious about romance and love in general, thanks to not having been exposed to [the television show] "The Love Boat" during their formative years. The more likely explanation, though, is that the anonymity of the medium, the prevalence of blogs, online photo galleries and personal Web sites, and the comfort most of us feel in corresponding entirely through e-mail have combined to make online dating a perfectly acceptable means of meeting new people.

Demand creates supply. When you think for a minute about how inefficient and circuitous the traditional delivery system for meeting potential lovers is, it's not hard to see how we landed here. When your options are limited to getting set up by your friends, going out to parties or going to smoky bars in the hopes of getting drunk enough to knock over someone with a pulse, it's clear why shopping for a mate online has been embraced by mainstream America.

> *We've entered a new era of self-branding, featuring tasty professional photographs and sales pitches feistier than those dreamt up by a skilled copywriter.*

Imagine, if you will, trying to buy a food processor without a Best Buy, or a Macy's, or a Williams-Sonoma. Imagine if you had to go to crowded parties and other tedious functions and search the crowd for someone with an old Cuisinart at home that they might be willing to sell you. Furthermore, imagine if it were considered rude to bring up the Cuisinart straight off the bat—instead, you were expected to ask people about themselves, maybe buy them a drink, and feign interest in their rambling, self-involved banter, until finally, at the end of the night, loosened up by a few drinks, you could say what had been on your mind for hours:

"Um. I hope this doesn't sound too forward, but do you . . . process food?"

And despite all that effort, imagine that the person's face drops, and he or she replies politely, but in a clipped, uncomfortable tone, "No, I'm not really into that kind of thing," and then exits the party without even asking for your number in case he or she ever does get the urge to process.

Now that love has finally been commodified and booty has an efficient distribution system, it makes sense that the branding strategies of those peddling their goods and services have become increasingly finessed.

Of course, it was only a matter of time before we gave up on classified ads and moved on to a more dynamic format. After all, how long could the same classy DWM ["divorced white male"], 50s, keep trumpeting his love for red wine and red roses and cuddling to any SWF ["straight white female"] who's both idle enough and disturbed enough to pore over that minuscule print? As Scott Bedbury, the marketing strategist who helped to launch campaigns for Nike and Starbucks, writes in his book, "A New Brand World":

> The most innovative product line will grow stale in the minds of potential consumers if the marketing has become static, undifferentiated, or—even worse—irritating for lack of change.

A change has certainly come upon us. Browse the personals on Bust.com or Nerve.com and you'll see for yourself: Gone are the candlelit dinners and the long walks on the beach. Cooking and travel and nights by the fire sound as old and lame as that "Like a Rock" theme song that Chevy can't seem to leave behind.

> **❝** *Since we've become products ourselves, it makes sense that we can only advertise ourselves by associating with other products.* **❞**

We've entered a new era of self-branding, featuring tasty professional photographs and sales pitches feistier than those dreamt up by a skilled copywriter. Today's online love-seeker isn't looking for someone who's "sexy and sophisticated and fit," he's looking for "Someone to end my hedonistic ways—or someone to take me headlong deeper into them." You can almost hear [pop singer] Britney [Spears] singing that bump-and-grind Pepsi theme song in the background: "The rrrride! Just enjoy the rrrride! Don't need a reason why!"

That jingle doesn't actually include the word "Pepsi," by the way—it's the natural evolution of ads that we move from an exhortation to consume the product ("Drink Pepsi!") to an invitation to enjoy a sensual experience that's only loosely (but inextricably) associated with the product ("Just enjoy the rrrride!"). Similarly, today's online ads are almost subliminal. What is he looking for? Not "a blue-eyed blond with a great rack." No! He's looking for "the connection, the compassion, the empathy and the acceptance we all seek." I had no idea [new age author] Deepak Chopra was single!

> *What does it mean to peddle yourself so effectively before you even meet your prospective partner? Can there possibly be any room left for the real, flawed, fragile human behind the ad?*

In keeping with current advertising trends, today's online singles market themselves not by highlighting their best traits, but by creating an imaginary self that's impressively snarky and carefree. Much like the recent spate of humorous TV ads for serious products like Washington Mutual or Budget Rent-a-Car, many personal ads use humor to draw in potential customers. For "Best (or worst) lie I've ever told," one guy wrote, "I never lie." And I found more than one straight man who listed *Deliverance* [which included a gay rape scene] as the source of his favorite on-screen sex scene.

Of course, Spring Street Networks deserves at least some of the credit for provoking participants into offering up such original and zesty prose. When "self-deprecation" is listed next to cigarettes and booze under "my habits," and you've asked to answer whether you indulge in it "often, sometimes, or never," the mind starts working in self-conscious yet creative new ways.

And who can't help but get a little clever or provocative when asked to fill in the following: "(blank) is sexy; (blank) is sexier." For example: "Flexibility is sexy; focus is sexier." Why not just say "Good sex is sexy; great sex is sexier"? Or how about this zinger: "Appearance is sexy; attitude is sexier." Sounds like the next Sprite campaign.

You have to hand it to these online daters for the enthusiasm with which they commodify themselves. Most seem unabashedly honest in exposing themselves, and few appear to be unfamiliar with the value-add. As Bedbury asserts, it's important to "know that your advertising must create a proposition that your product or service delivers on, time and time again."

Accordingly, chirpy love-seekers offer up their services with the enthusiasm of merchants at a street market: "I visit the beach or the canyons at least once a week!" "I'm easy-going and intense!" "I give great massages!". . .

Furthermore, Bedbury explains, the great brands tell a story, like a great piece of mythology, "with the customer, not the company, as the story's main protagonist." Our online love-seekers seem to sense this intuitively: "[You're] not someone who thinks [the cartoon] *Cathy* is funny, but someone who thinks *The Jerk* is funny." "You love who you are, but you want so much more." "You'll love my vegan pancakes in the morning!"

> **"** *Navigating today's online personals can feel more like an exercise in fantasy: We take the artifacts before us, and use our powers of imagination to create an idealized mate from these offerings.* **"**

And since we've become products ourselves, it makes sense that we can only advertise ourselves by associating with other products. Indeed, each personal ad patches together an increasingly eclectic and romantic mélange of brands to create a signature brand. . . . The cultural references become dizzying after a while, with each brand standing on the shoulders of a million brands that came before it. . . .

But as online ads become more aggressive and clever and self-consciously crafted, what impact does that have on the human interactions that result from them? What does it mean to peddle yourself so effectively before you even meet your prospective partner? Can there possibly be any room left for the real, flawed, fragile human behind the ad?

And after buying into the suave vegan pancake-maker and cognac-sipping reader of [poet Walt] Whitman, can you possibly accept the humble, nervous accountant who stands before you? With such a marketing blitz, followed by frisky, flirtatious instant messaging and countless e-mails, followed sometimes even by long midnight conversations and phone sex, is it remotely possible not to be disappointed with the real thing?

Like reading a book and then seeing the movie, you don't realize how much you've already painted a picture in your head until you see someone else's vision on the screen. Similarly, it's tough to know how much fantasy you're bringing to the table until you're sitting face to face, and you recognize suddenly that you'd ascribed a whole different set of verbal tics, affectations and gestures to the person in your mind without even knowing it.

The smallest thing about the person can send you spiraling inward, thereby shutting you off from the experience. You felt sure, based on his e-mails, that he wasn't a mouth breather! It seemed obvious, given the flirtatious confidence with which she approached you online, that she didn't have a flabby ass!

In "A New Brand World," Bedbury quotes University of Michigan business professors C.K. Prahalad and Venkatram Ramaswamy who contend that a "product is no more than an artifact around which customers have experiences." Similarly, navigating today's online personals can feel more like an exercise in fantasy: We take the artifacts before us, and use our powers of imagination to create an idealized mate from these offerings.

Strange how easy and familiar this process is to us; but then, most relationships are at least 30 percent imagination. Without a fantasy-driven notion of themselves as a pair, most couples' relationships would collapse under the weight of years of compromise and self-sacrifice.

And besides, for as long as I've known her, my online dating friend in New York has been lamenting that she never meets any new men—ever! Now she meets them all the time. They're not all perfect, and sometimes she's built them up in her mind only to be disappointed. But now at least she's getting out there and hanging out with new people, and for better or for worse, she says she has a real feeling of possibility.

"I might have stayed involved with the last guy even though it wasn't working, because I would've thought, I'll never meet anyone else!" she says. "Now I know I can just go online and meet someone else tomorrow." That's right. There are always more brands on the shelf—I mean, fish in the sea.

8

Internet Dating Could Improve Relationships and Marriage

Valerie Reitman

Valerie Reitman is a staff writer for the Los Angeles Times, *where she frequently writes on health and lifestyle issues.*

New Internet dating services use sophisticated personality, lifestyle, and values tests to match users to prospective mates. In many ways online dating is superior to more traditional forms of dating because it allows participants to connect by learning about one another's values and beliefs rather than relying on serendipity or superficial judgments. Thousands of couples have already gotten married due to Internet dating services, and many new users sign up every day. No longer regarded as a last resort for the desperate, online dating is becoming increasingly popular as its utility is recognized.

L onely after his wife of 46 years died in 2000, Roger Moore, 75, tried Internet dating but quickly grew tired of prospective dates' self-promotional profiles. The "on-line meat market," as he called it, consisted primarily of details such as would-be dates' hair and eye color and their affinities for sunset walks on the beach. The descriptions were short on the things that mattered: personality, character and shared values.

So when Moore heard a radio advertisement for Eharmony .com—an online dating company that promised help in finding a soul mate based on personality assessments—he paid $250 for a yearlong membership.

The retired Los Alamos nuclear laboratory statistician answered the 436 questions in the personality profile, ranging from how much he enjoyed playing pranks on others to how agreeable and frugal he was. On a scale of 1 to 7, was he dominant? Cold? Gregarious? Desirous of sexual activity?

As the stigma of online dating as a last resort fades, millions of U.S. singles of all ages are trying to find mates via a click of a mouse. But with hundreds of thousands of paying subscribers, some of the most popular sites are adding elaborate psychological tests—such as Eharmony.com's—to match people with those they might get along with best.

Measuring Personality Types

The online dating companies have hired psychologists and computer experts to refine questionnaires not only to hone their knowledge about what personality types are mostly likely to click, but also to determine the most important elements each subscriber is looking for in a match.

Pasadena-based Eharmony.com started the trend four years ago with its 29-areas-of-compatibility index. At least in part because of Eharmony's popularity, others, such as TrueBeginnings, have followed suit with their own personality assessments. TrueBeginnings also runs its subscribers through a database of convicted felons—rapsheets.com—to weed out potential stalkers or thieves.

Even Match.com, which pioneered online dating in 1995 and boasts the largest number of visitors to its site, has begun offering an eight-minute personality test and has gone as far as developing a physical attraction test to help determine what physical traits are most appealing to each individual—for instance, men who tend to be lean and angular, ones with square jaws or those who resemble "bears" because of their large sizes and gentle nature.

It soon plans to screen potential dates' photos, presenting subscribers with ones who seem to be their type, both physically and mentally.

In Moore's case, Eharmony.com's computers spat back 100 potential matches with similar traits, of which Moore met six in person. But none seemed to be "the one." He widened his geographical scope, and a tantalizing prospect arrived in his inbox: Barbara, a retired physical therapist, also 75 and widowed after an equally long marriage.

They traded e-mails, gabbed on the phone and finally arranged to meet at Spiffy's restaurant—halfway between their respective Vancouver and Sammanish, Wash., homes. For the next date, he drove the 180 miles for a lunch at her house, and she mentioned that her spare bedroom was available for his next visit.

They married in February, their six middle-aged children serving as attendants.

As Moore found, online matchmaking tools can be quite helpful, serving at least as a starting point. Outside of meeting someone at school or work, the odds of finding a compatible date or mate through more traditional methods—at singles bars, via introductions by mutual friends or by sheer serendipity—are mostly random and inefficient, social scientists say.

"People are not good at understanding what they find attractive in other people," said Aaron Ahuvia, a consumer psychologist and associate professor of marketing at the University of Michigan, who has studied dating behavior. "People tend to focus on common interests and superficial characteristics and not understand the importance of—or want to talk about—goals, values and what they want to get out of a relationship."

> *As the stigma of online dating as a last resort fades, millions of U.S. singles of all ages are trying to find mates via a click of a mouse.*

Advance screening can increase the odds that two people will like and be compatible with each other, Ahuvia says—and save the substantial amount of time that might be invested before one would otherwise broach potentially deal-breaking concerns such as whether the other person wanted kids.

The profiles can be a good way of narrowing the field from, say, 10,000 candidates to 10 and then figuring which of those might be worth getting to know.

The personality assessments—and computer matching—can also be helpful in overcoming the emphasis on looks, which (particularly for men) plays a big part in the search. "If the computer says you should look at this person—even if they don't look like your ideal—hopefully, you'd be generous enough to give it a try," Ahuvia says.

But letting the computer pick matches might also prevent subscribers from reviewing candidates who, for whatever reason, they might not be matched with—but who could still be ideal. (Match.com lets subscribers review all candidates; Eharmony and TrueBeginnings do not.)

Similarities and Differences

Each company has its own formula. Eharmony weighs similarities as most important, incorporating founder Neil Clark Warren's observations from the 35 years he spent as a psychologist, counseling thousands of couples trying to repair failing marriages. The happiest couples, in his experience, tend to be of similar intelligence, energy, ambition and industriousness, with lots of common interests and things they enjoy doing together.

> *Outside of . . . school or work, the odds of finding a compatible date or mate through more traditional methods . . . are mostly random and inefficient, social scientists say.*

"Similarities are like money in the bank," says Warren, who has been happily married for 45 years to his wife, Marylyn, a senior vice president at the company. "Differences are like debts you owe. It's all right to have a few debts as long as you have equity in the bank; otherwise you go bankrupt."

Moreover, he says, other things—such as sharing religion or spirituality, wanting or not wanting to have children—are weighted based on how important those factors are to each individual. One particularly important measure of compatibility, he notes, seems to be whether two people share a passion for the arts. It's fine if neither does, but if one does and the other doesn't, it could be a big problem.

Of course, Warren says, strong couples can sustain some differences. He and wife Marylyn, for instance, have opposite political views and argued vehemently during the days following the last presidential election [2000], when the outcome was in dispute for weeks. "If we didn't have so much equity in our

72

account when the Gore-Bush thing was going on in Florida, it would have ripped at us," Warren said.

Many of the other services also weigh heavily similar interests and shared values. In general, most social scientists say, while opposites might initially attract, over time they repel.

TrueBeginnings takes a somewhat different view. It connects subscribers based not only on the characteristics they share and desire in a mate, but also on some of the differences that might improve their relationship. For example, if one person handles money management poorly, the last person he or she should be paired with is someone with that same trait.

But such complementary differences can turn into a liability if the relationship deteriorates; the one handling the money, for instance, might be viewed as controlling rather than helpful.

James Houran, TrueBeginnings' director of psychological studies, says the cement in the relationship comes from how much the pair enjoy and are committed to each other and the relationship—and that element is what tests can't measure.

WeAttract.com, which developed the personality test for Match.com, takes the view that "lasting relationships are those that can live with quirks—and those that might even make the partner more adorable to the other," says Mark Thompson, president of WeAttract.com and developer of the test.

"Most of us are 6 or 7s (on a scale of 10), so maybe they're not an A but really a B. But we want to be with someone who thinks we're an A," he adds. "The beautiful thing about the Internet is that even if that person [who appreciates you] is one in a million, you can find [that person]."

He recalls a Rubenesque [full-figured] woman some years ago whom he thought was beautiful—but who complained that no one wanted to date her. If Internet dating were available back then, she likely would have found plenty of men who appreciated her beauty and personality.

Proceeding with Caution

Still, even finding people who seem on paper to be compatible doesn't mean they'll find chemistry when they get together. No one has been able to figure out why one is drawn to one person and not another.

Says Warren, "Do I understand attraction—is it chemical? Is it olfactory, is it aesthetic? I don't care how compatible you are, if there's no chemistry, don't seal the thing: Love minus chemistry equals friendship. Don't try to turn it into love."

Moreover, people often start out with inherent biases that some services have incorporated into their formulas, because after all, it is a business that aims to satisfy its customers. For example, Eharmony.com only matches women with taller men—because so many women complain if they're set up with shorter men, says Warren. And 25% of men older than 50 say they only want to be set up with "fertile" women—that is, younger women in their 20s and 30s, Warren says.

Men are so visual, Warren said, that they demand to see pictures with matches—which he would rather have revealed in the latter stages of communication rather than the preliminary stages. (They can be revealed—if a subscriber chooses to post one—after each determines that they want to communicate with the other match.)

Some people try to outwit the tests to make themselves look better, but services with comprehensive profiles try to screen them out by asking similar questions repeatedly to get at the truth. Eharmony says it also rejects thousands of would-be subscribers who indicate they are depressed or have addiction problems. Warren says people need to be in control and relatively happy in their own lives before they can be good partners.

> *The [online dating] personality assessments . . . can also be helpful in overcoming the emphasis on looks, which (particularly for men) plays a large part in the search.*

The Eharmony.com test takes about an hour and, by the end, can feel tedious. And that's just the beginning. Once all the primary information is on the table, the pair communicate via Eharmony's e-mail system several times, answering each other's questions. If all goes well, the next step is meeting in person and determining—within at most two dates, Warren says—whether the person is just a "Date . . . or Soul Mate?," the title of Warren's book that comes with a membership.

Mara Adelman, an associate professor of communications and a social psychologist at Seattle University, says this "date data-dumping" is too much, too fast, too soon.

"That initial hour—when you're trying to assess whether the person is going to be the father of your child—you're dumping a tremendous amount of data, where there is no context for the disclosure," she says. "It puts a lot of pressure on the situation, and you don't have any history or context to put it in."

> *Eharmony says 2,500 marriages can be linked directly to its site so far, though [founder Neil Clark] Warren estimates there have been 10 times that many since the company was started [in 2000].*

Instead, she says, information should be shared over time—when one can see how a date interacts with friends and get a chance to really know him.

Success Stories

It remains to be seen whether marriages and relationships determined with the help of a computer algorithm will last longer than more traditional arrangements.

Eharmony says 2,500 marriages can be linked directly to its site so far, though Warren estimates there have been 10 times that many since the company was started [in 2000].

Still, if the sentiments of six couples matched by Eharmony and interviewed recently are any indication, it's not a bad start. They all seemed very much in love, finishing each other's sentences, touching and bragging about how they seemed to be soul mates.

To be sure, maybe they are the giddiest of the giddy: Most had written Eharmony to gush about how they'd found their true loves on the site. Eharmony paid their airfare and hotel accommodations (including separate rooms for the not-yet-married couples) to bring them to Santa Monica for a professional photo shoot for future ads and to interview them for radio spots.

One benefit, agreed Cheryl and Patrick Winning, is that the personality profile helps not only in understanding their partners better, but also in helping the individuals better understand themselves and what they need in the relationship.

Most of those interviewed thought the personality assessments represented their strengths and weaknesses fairly well.

The Winnings married in January [2004] after Eharmony matched them late last summer. (He got 212 matches, she got five—testament to the fact that Eharmony has 60% women and 40% male members. The older and more educated a person is—particularly the woman—the harder she is to match, Warren says.)

Patrick Winning, a divorce attorney, says he knows "all the pitfalls" of marriage. The primary factors he sees in his divorcing clients are inability to communicate and inability to manage conflict.

He also knows from personal experience: He was divorced after a two-decade marriage, as was his new wife, Cheryl. But how well could they possibly know each other after dating less than five months in which they only saw each other on weekends because he lived in St. Louis and she lived 300 miles away in Louisville?

Because of the tests and their upfront discussions, Cheryl Winning said, "I felt I knew more about Patrick than I did [my previous husband], and I was married for 21 years."

The six couples also said they had developed passion after finding they had common ground. "It was very comfortable," said Roger Moore. "That transition from the formality to the informality was very straightforward. And besides," he adds, "I love her."

9

The Internet Could Exacerbate the Gap Between Rich and Poor Nations

Ashfaq Ishaq

Ashfaq Ishaq is founder of the International Child Art Foundation (ICAF), which encourages creativity and world peace by teaching art skills to underserved children worldwide. He holds a PhD in economics from George Washington University and frequently writes on global economic issues.

The Internet holds great promise to improve human life, but at the present time only a small percentage of people worldwide can access it. The fear of a global society divided into two classes—an affluent, technologically skilled minority and a poorer, technologically backward majority—is realistic. Governments and global relief organizations have both a moral responsibility to respond to this "digital divide" before it becomes a long-term trend. The Internet stands to dramatically improve the economies of impoverished countries worldwide, provided access can be improved.

The digital and information revolution presents a historic opportunity for developing countries to take a quantum leap forward, develop their own productive and creative capacities, and become integrated into the global virtual economy. However, Internet density (users as a percentage of popu-

Ashfaq Ishaq, "On the Global Digital Divide," *Finance and Development*, vol. 38, September 2001, p. 44. Copyright © 2001 by *Finance and Development*. Reproduced by permission of International Monetary Fund, conveyed through Copyright Clearance Center, Inc.

lation) is still much higher in industrial countries, as well as in affluent and educated communities in every country, than elsewhere. The Internet threatens to magnify the existing socioeconomic disparities, between those with access and those without, to levels unseen and untenable. Therefore, urgent actions are needed at the local, national, and international levels to bridge the global digital divide. This article outlines both the digital opportunity and the digital divide and argues that bridging the divide is a precondition for a worldwide creativity revolution to blossom.

The Big Divide

In the final pages of Jacques Barzun's opus [*From Dawn to Decadence*] on the past five hundred years of Western cultural life, he conjures up the following vision of the year 2300:

> The population was divided into two groups; they did not like the word classes. The first, less numerous, was made up of the men and women who possessed the virtually inborn ability to handle the products of techne and master the methods of physical science, especially mathematics—it was to them what Latin had been to medieval clergy. This modern elite had the geometric mind that singled them out for the life of research and engineering. ... Dials, toggles, buzzers, gauges, icons on screens, light-emitting diodes, symbols and formulas to save time and thought—these were for this group of people the source of emotional satisfaction, the means to rule over others, the substance of shoptalk, the very joy and justification of life. . . . It is from this class—no, group—that the governors and heads of institutions are recruited. The parallel with the Middle Ages is plain—clerics in one case, cybernists in the other. The latter took pride in the fact that in ancient Greek cybernetes means helmsman, governor. It validated their position as rulers over the masses, which by then could neither read nor count. But these less capable citizens were by no means barbarians, yet any schooling would have been wasted on them; that had been proved in the late [twentieth century]. Some now argue that the schooling was at fault, not the pupils; but

when the teachers themselves declared children unteachable, the Deschooling Society movement rapidly converted everyone to its view.

This is Barzun's description of the digital divide, written as if it were being viewed from after the year 2300 but actually reflecting New York's reality in 1995—just before the Internet created the greatest equity wealth boom in the history of mankind. At present, the digital divide mirrors the technology gap separating the rich countries from the poor ones—a gap that opened up during the industrial revolution and has yet to be fully bridged. The pessimistic view of the digital divide—that it is widening as information and communications technologies (ICTs) advance to broadband—is likely to prevail if the public, private, and civil sectors fail to bridge it before it becomes too expansive and intractable.

> *The Internet threatens to magnify the existing socioeconomic disparities, between those with access and those without, to levels unseen and untenable.*

The uncontested fact is that the Internet is still growing at a phenomenal pace. Estimating the current number of Internet users is difficult, however, because one person may have multiple Internet accounts or a single account may have multiple users. . . . More than 400 million users were online in November 2000, with nearly 69 percent of them in the United States, Canada, and Europe. Internet density has increased to more than 53 percent in the United States and Canada, but is a mere 1 percent in the Middle East and 0.4 percent in Africa. Overall, a modest 7 percent of the world's population uses the Internet, which shows both how widely the Internet has spread and how much remains to be done before universal access is attained.

Universal Access

Access requires an Internet device, such as a personal computer (PC), electricity, telephone service, and an Internet service provider (ISP). Today, there is virtually no technological constraint preventing access; even a remote village or a faraway hamlet lacking both telephones and electricity can be connected to the Internet using a satellite dish and solar power. The constraint, therefore, is purely financial. At the local level, the costs of building the necessary infrastructure and procuring the equipment have to be financed. At the national level, the foreign exchange cost of importing needed equipment and services must be met. At the international level, a funding mechanism to promote universal access has to be established.

> *Universal [Internet] access must be defined, ideally, as a basic necessity, if not a right.*

To begin with, universal access must be defined, ideally, as a basic necessity, if not a right. The trend in industrial countries is to guarantee access anywhere, anytime, through multiple devices. Students, for example, can connect to the Internet at their schools or homes or at libraries, community centers, or shopping malls. Further, wireless technology is making the Internet nearly omnipresent. Poor countries cannot afford such an array of choices, however. In most villages and towns, only a single central access point can be established. Examples of such shared access are community cyber centers in Jamaica, mobile Net units in Asia, Internet cafes in South America, cyber bars in Eastern Europe, e-mail kiosks in India, and walk-in Internet posts in Mongolia.

Although in industrial countries the distance between users and Internet-ready computers is nearly zero, in developing countries it can be several miles. Shared access and the acceptance of the "last mile" between an average user and the nearest access point can drastically reduce per capita access costs. Universal access can be further refined to mean that one member of every family anywhere has access to the Web for at least a short period every day or every week. Through this single online member, the entire family can be occasionally connected to the virtual world, enabling it to reap some of the benefits of the digital revolution. Universal access, thus narrowly defined, may be possible by 2005, as has been advocated by the United Nations.

More optimistically, Internet users have increased by about 100 million a year in the past couple of years. If this rate continues, the population online will increase from 400 million in 2000 to 900 million in 2005. However, bringing each successive 100 million people online will require greater and greater financial and training resources.

With four billion unique, indexable pages already, the Internet offers incredible and unprecedented communications, learning, and transaction opportunities for those connected to the Web. Without adequate training, however, users cannot employ the Internet effectively to advance their own objectives. Instead, they may find themselves lost on the Web, as a result of information overload, or get caught in the net of pirates, perverts, and impostors.

When the Internet's local impact grows, it will become more attractive to new users, who will be predominantly from the developing world. Although the Internet started as a U.S.-centric medium, and English continues to dominate the Web, the publication of local content is gaining momentum and support. A report of the Digital Opportunity Task Force (DOT Force) established at the 2000 Group of Eight Summit in Kyushu-Okinawa (Group of Eight, 2000) states

> Innovative partnerships are required to support local content creation and dissemination, including indigenous knowledge preservation. A key aspect of this is the creation of the technical foundations for greater cultural/linguistic diversity on the Internet, including better integration of different writing systems with the Net's technical standards. . . .
> A related priority is technical and financial support for content-development tools for non-literate populations, to enhance not only effective use of ICTs but also the cultural diversity of content available online.

Implementation of these recommendations will enrich the Internet and enhance its national usefulness.

Online Education and Economic Development

Several major universities, including Massachusetts Institute of Technology Cambridge, are placing their course materials online, making them available to all. More significantly, the Internet is bringing about a revolution in learning and education. New approaches are taking root and spreading, involving radical changes in attitudes as well as incorporation of new research on how learning takes place and how to make education more effective. The Internet is replacing the "sage on the stage" pattern of instruction with a new model of "guide on the side." With students at the center of the learning process, schools can become fundamental agents for change, helping reengineer the whole educational system and stimulating lifelong learning.

The Internet is a place not only to acquire knowledge but also to create, document, and store it. Users are coming together to create knowledge networks and "mutual education communities." E-mentoring on the Web is possible through listservs, connecting students on one continent with tutors on another. In sum, the Internet has opened exciting new opportunities for human capital development, which can and should result in a more informed, empowered, and creative citizenry— a precondition for economic development.

A growing recognition of the Internet as a promising path for economic development of poor countries has led to e-development—the pursuit of new opportunities available to those with access to the Internet. Here again, closing the digital divide becomes a primary concern. The hope is that e-development will not consist merely of the publication of old recipes in a new medium. Rather, it would usher in new theories and practices of economic development. As Jack Welch, the Chairman of General Electric, has famously stated: "The secret of success is changing the way you think."

> *The Internet has opened exciting new opportunities for human capital development, which can and should result in a more informed, empowered, and creative citizenry—a precondition for economic development.*

Meanwhile, the development landscape is rapidly changing: taxpayers in Brazil can file their tax returns online; farmers in Bhutan access the Web to learn how to protect their harvest and improve crop yields; radio talk-show hosts in Sri Lanka surf the Net in response to questions and air the answers in local languages; nurses in Gambian villages use digital cameras to download and transfer images of patients' symptoms to nearby towns for examination by doctors; when Hurricane Mitch hit Honduras in 1998, the Internet helped expedite and broaden the relief efforts; and the same year Timbuktu, Mali, went on-line. Every week, a new community in Africa, Asia, or Latin America gets connected to the Web, publishes its own website, starts e-commerce, or embraces e-learning. All such projects need to be supported, promoted, and replicated with national and international assistance, because the more widespread the digital opportunity becomes, the greater will be the incentive at local levels to gain access to the Web.

> *Every week, a new community in Africa, Asia, or Latin America gets connected to the Web, publishes its own website, starts e-commerce, or embraces e-learning.*

With universal access and an Internet-literate workforce, the digital revolution can serve as the engine of economic growth and development. To this end, it is necessary to create ICT ministries that deal specifically with complex Internet issues, ranging from privacy to taxation. Internet ministers would benefit from an IMF [International Monetary Fund]- or World Bank–sponsored listserv through which they can exchange ideas and collaborate. This could be a first step in creating a virtual community of political, corporate, and civil society leaders to address the global digital divide.

The Creativity Revolution

Starting as a new medium for communication and information, the Internet has quickly become a place for learning and transactions. The initial impact of the Net has been on increasing productivity in the workplace. For example, the use of ICT contributed close to 50 percent of the total acceleration in U.S. productivity in the second half of the 1990s (United States Internet Council, 2000). Wireless technology will further increase productivity by allowing individuals to make effective use of the time they have available between tasks. And there is much more to come, considering that the digital revolution is still in its infancy.

The full promise of the digital revolution lies in the blossoming of a creativity revolution worldwide. The Internet can be a dynamic platform for the use of knowledge through new forms of learning, so that individuals and organizations can achieve their creative potential. Already, there is a growing awareness that creativity should be a central focus of public policy. A [2001] paper on U.S. cultural policy [by Shalini Venturelli] warns that "a culture persists in time only to . . . [the] degree it is inventing, creating, and dynamically evolving in a way that promotes the production of ideas across all social classes and groups." Indeed, without creative dynamism, seemingly productive societies fade away, leaving behind their rusted factories and social detritus. Developing creative capacities is hence the defining challenge for individuals, organizations, societies, and governments.

The new growth theorists' introduction of ideas and knowledge as inputs in the production equation reflects a recognition that the new economy is a creative economy, characterized by high potential output growth and low inflationary expectations. A [2000] book titled *The Ingenuity Gap* discusses the gap between the difficulty of the problems faced by societies (the demand for ingenuity) and the delivery of ideas in response to these problems (the supply of ingenuity). A creativity revolution can ensure that new ideas are generated in time to avoid diminishing returns on investment and that ingenuity is present to solve problems along the way.

A creativity divide has existed in the world since long before there was a digital divide or a technology gap. The digital revolution can finally close the creativity divide by fostering and supporting human creativity worldwide. For this to occur, however, the global digital divide needs to be bridged and the Internet's potential to serve as a creativity playground for children needs to be harnessed. This would ensure that the next generation is more imaginative, innovative, creative, and artistic.

Because the digital and information revolution is still in its infancy, it is impossible to predict whether this revolution will ultimately provide a unique opportunity for the poor to leapfrog into prosperity or whether the digital divide will deepen with time, relegating a majority of the world's population to a technological underclass that will be held back for generations to come. At its best, the digital revolution can blossom into a creativity revolution. At its worst, it will pit the cybernists against the unschooled majority in a battle without end.

10

The Internet Will Threaten and Protect Privacy

David F. Brin

David F. Brin is a freelance writer. Among his fifty-eight books—many of them bestselling science fiction novels—is the nonfiction book The Transparent Society *(1999), winner of the American Library Association's Freedom of Speech Award. It deals with the question of how technology might change existing notions of privacy.*

The Internet has made surveillance technology more practical by making it possible to link data together in global networks. The effects are already being felt today—England, for example, has over 1 million networked police cameras—and as surveillance technology becomes more sophisticated, less expensive, and more easily available, privacy as it is defined today will continue to erode. Although many believe that surveillance technology can simply be banned, history has proven otherwise. As soon as technology is available cheaply, it will almost certainly be used. The best option will be for citizens to use the same technologies that governments use to observe and hold accountable their public officials.

Ten centuries ago, at the previous millennium, a Viking lord commanded the rising tide to retreat. No deluded fool, King Canute aimed in this way to teach flatterers a lesson—that even sovereign rulers cannot halt inexorable change.

A thousand years later, we face tides of technology-driven

David F. Brin, "Three Cheers for the Surveillance Society!" Salon.com, August 3, 2004. This article first appeared in Salon.com, at www.Salon.com. An online version remains in the Salon archives. Reprinted with permission.

transformation that seem bound only to accelerate. Waves of innovation may liberate human civilization, or disrupt it, more than anything since glass lenses and movable type. Critical decisions during the next few years—about research, investment, law and lifestyle—may determine what kind of civilization our children inherit. Especially problematic are many information-related technologies that loom on the near horizon—technologies that may foster tyranny, or else empower citizenship in a true global village.

Typically we are told, often and passionately, that Big Brother[1] may abuse these new powers. Or else our privacy and rights will be violated by some other group. Perhaps a commercial, aristocratic, bureaucratic, intellectual, foreign, criminal or technological elite. (Pick your favorite bogeyman.)

Because one or more of these centers of power might use the new tools to see better, we're told that we should all be very afraid. Indeed, our only hope may be to squelch or fiercely control the onslaught of change. For the sake of safety and liberty, we are offered one prescription: We must limit the power of others to see.

> *Critical decisions during the next few years—about research, investment, law, and lifestyle—may determine what kind of civilization our children inherit.*

Half a century ago, amid an era of despair, George Orwell created one of the most oppressive metaphors in literature with the telescreen system used to surveil and control the people in his novel *1984*. We have been raised to a high degree of sensitivity by Orwell's *self-preventing* prophecy, and others like it. Attuned to wariness, today's activists preach that any growth in the state's ability to see will take us down a path of no return, toward the endless hell of Big Brother.

But consider. The worst aspect of Orwell's telescreen—the trait guaranteeing tyranny—was not that agents of the state could use it to see. The one thing that despots truly need is to avoid accountability. In *1984*, this is achieved by keeping the

1. the fictional oppressive government described in George Orwell's novel *1984*

telescreen aimed in just one direction! By preventing the people from looking back.

While a flood of new discoveries may seem daunting, they should not undermine the core values of a calm and knowledgeable citizenry. Quite the opposite: While privacy may have to be redefined, the new technologies of surveillance should and will be the primary countervailing force against tyranny.

In any event, none of those who denounce the new technologies have shown how it will be possible to stop this rising tide.

Radio Chips

Consider a few examples:

Radio frequency identification (RFID) technology will soon replace the simple, passive bar codes on packaged goods, substituting inexpensive chips that respond to microwave interrogation, making every box of toothpaste or razor blades part of a vast, automatic inventory accounting system. Wal-Mart announced in 2003 that it will require its top 100 suppliers to use RFID on all large cartons, for purposes of warehouse inventory keeping. But that is only the beginning. Inevitably as prices fall, RFID chips will be incorporated into most products and packaging.

Supermarket checkout will become a breeze, when you simply push your cart past a scanner and grab a printout receipt, with every purchase automatically debited from your account.

> *While privacy may have to be redefined, the new technologies of surveillance should and will be the primary countervailing force against tyranny.*

Does that sound simultaneously creepy and useful? Well, it goes much further. Under development are smart washers that will read the tags on clothing and adjust their cycles accordingly, and smart medicine cabinets that track tagged prescriptions, in order to warn which ones have expired or need refilling. Cars and desks and computers will adjust to your preferred settings as you approach. Paramedics may download your health status—

including allergies and dangerous drug-conflicts—even if you are unconscious or unable to speak.

There's a downside. A wonderful 1960s paranoia satire, *The President's Analyst*, offered prophetic warning against implanted devices, inserted into people, that would allow them to be tracked by big business and government. But who needs implantation when your clothing and innocuous possessions will carry cheap tags of their own that can be associated with their owners? Already some schools—especially in Asia—are experimenting with RFID systems that will locate all students, at all times.

Oh, there will be fun to be had, for a while, in fooling these systems with minor acts of irreverent rebellion. Picture kids swapping clothes and possessions, furtively, in order to leave muddled trails. Still, such measures will not accomplish much over extended periods. Tracking on vast scales, national and worldwide, will emerge in rapid order. And if we try to stop it with legislation, the chief effect will only be to drive the surveillance into secret networks that are just as pervasive. Only they will operate at levels we cannot supervise, study, discuss or understand.

Wait, there's more. For example, a new Internet protocol (IPv6) will vastly expand available address space in the virtual world.

> *Supermarket checkout will become a breeze, when you simply push your cart past a scanner and grab a printout receipt, with every purchase automatically debited from your account.*

The present IP, offering 32-bit data labels, can now offer every living human a unique online address, limiting direct access to something like 10 billion Web pages or specific computers. In contrast, IPv6 will use 128 bits. This will allow the virtual tagging of every cubic centimeter of the earth's surface, from sea level to mountaintop, spreading a multidimensional data overlay across the planet. Every tagged or manmade object may participate, from your wristwatch to a nearby lamppost, vending machine or trash can—even most of the discarded contents of the trash can.

Every interest group will find some kind of opportunity in this new world. Want to protect forests? Each and every tree on earth might have a chip fired into its bark from the air, alerting a network if furtive loggers start transporting stolen hardwoods. Or the same method could track whoever steals your morning paper. Not long after this, teens and children will purchase rolls of ultra-cheap digital eyes and casually stick them onto walls. Millions of those "penny cams" will join in the fun, contributing to the vast IPv6 datasphere.

> *When your car recognizes your face, and all the stores can verify your fingerprint, what need will you have for keys or a credit card?*

Oh, this new Internet protocol will offer many benefits—for example, embedded systems for data tracking and verification. In the short term, expanded powers of vision *may* embolden tyrants. But over the long run, these systems could help to empower citizens and enhance mutual trust.

Millions of Cameras

In the mid-'90s, when I began writing *The Transparent Society*, it seemed dismaying to note that Great Britain had almost 150,000 police cameras scanning public streets. Today, they number in the millions.

In the United States, a similar proliferation, though just as rapid, has been somewhat masked by a different national tradition—that of dispersed ownership. As pointed out by [University of California]–San Diego researcher Mohan Trivedi, American constabularies have few cameras of their own. Instead, they rely on vast numbers of security monitors operated by small and large companies, banks, markets and private individuals, who scan ever larger swaths of urban landscape. Nearly all of the footage that helped solve the Oklahoma City bombing and the D.C. sniper episode—as well as documenting the [September 11, 2001, terrorist attacks]—came from unofficial sources.

This unique system can be both effective and inexpensive for state agencies, especially when the public is inclined to cooperate, as in searches for missing children. Still, there are many irksome drawbacks to officials who may want more pervasive and direct surveillance. For one thing, the present method relies upon high levels of mutual trust and goodwill between authorities and the owners of those cameras—whether they be convenience-store corporations or videocam-equipped private citizens. Moreover, while many crimes are solved with help from private cameras, more police are also held accountable for well-documented lapses in professional behavior.

This tattletale trend began with the infamous beating of [black man] Rodney King [by white police officers], more than a decade ago, and has continued at an accelerating pace. Among recently exposed events were those that aroused disgust (the tormenting of live birds in the Pilgrim's Pride slaughterhouse) and shook America's stature in the world (the prisoner abuse by jailers at Abu Ghraib prison in Iraq). Each time the lesson is the same one: that professionals should attend to their professionalism, or else the citizens and consumers who pay their wages will find out and—eventually—hold them accountable.

(Those wishing to promote the trend might look into [the nonprofit organization] Project Witness which supplies cameras to underdogs around the world.)

Will American authorities decide to abandon this quaint social bargain of shared access to sensors under dispersed ownership? As the price of electronic gear plummets, it will become easy and cheap for our professional protectors to purchase their own dedicated systems of surveillance, like those already operating in Britain, Singapore and elsewhere. Systems that "look down from above" (surveillance) without any irksome public involvement.

The End of Anonymity

Or might authorities simply use our networks without asking? A decade ago, the U.S. government fought activist groups such as the Electronic Frontier Foundation, claiming a need to unlock commercial-level encryption codes at will, for the sake of law enforcement and national defense. Both sides won apparent victories. High-level commercial encryption became widely available. And the government came to realize that it doesn't matter. It never did.

Shall I go on?

Driven partly by security demands, a multitude of biometric technologies will identify individuals by scanning physical attributes, from fingerprints, iris patterns, faces and voices to brainwaves and possibly unique chemical signatures. Starting with those now entering and leaving the United States, whole classes of people will grow accustomed to routine identification in this way. Indeed, citizens may start to demand more extensive use of biometric identification, as a safety measure against identity theft. When your car recognizes your face, and all the stores can verify your fingerprint, what need will you have for keys or a credit card?

> *With so many identification methodologies working independently and in parallel, our children may find the word 'anonymous' impossibly quaint.*

Naturally, this is yet another trend that has put privacy activists in a lather. They worry—with some justification—about civil liberties implications when the police or FBI might scan multitudes (say, at a sporting event) in search of fugitives or suspects. Automatic software agents will recognize individuals who pass through one camera view, then perform a smooth handoff to the next camera, and the next, planting a "tail" on dozens, hundreds, or tens of thousands of people at a time.

And yes, without a doubt this method could become a potent tool for some future Big Brother.

So? Should that legitimate and plausible fear be addressed by reflexively blaming technology and seeking ways to restrict its use? Or by finding ways that technology may work for us, instead of against us?

Suppose you could ban or limit a particular identification technique. (Mind you, I've seen no evidence that it can be done.) The sheer number of different, overlapping biometric approaches will make that whole approach fruitless. In fact, human beings fizz and froth with unique traits that can be spotted at a glance, even with our old-fashioned senses. Our ancestors relied on this fact, building and correlating lists of people who merited trust or worry, from among the few thousands that they met in person. In a global village of 10 billion souls, machines will do the same thing for us by prosthetically amplifying vision and augmenting memory.

With so many identification methodologies working independently and in parallel, our children may find the word "anonymous" impossibly quaint, perhaps even incomprehensible. But that needn't mean an end to freedom—or even privacy. Although it will undoubtedly mean a redefinition of what we think privacy means.

Data, Data Everywhere

But onward with our scan of panopticonic technologies. Beyond RFID, IPv6 and biometrics there are smart cards, smart highways, smart airports, smart automobiles, smart televisions, smart homes and so on.

The shared adjective may be premature. These systems will provide improved service long before anything like actual "artificial intelligence" comes online. Yet machinery needn't be strictly intelligent in order to transform our lives. Moreover, distributed "smart" units will also gather information, joining together in cross-correlating networks that recognize travelers, perform security checks, negotiate micro-transactions, detect criminal activity, warn of potential danger and anticipate desires. When these parts fully interlink, the emerging entity may not be self-aware, but it will certainly know the whereabouts of its myriad parts.

> *In the future, you can assume that almost any electronic device will be trackable, though citizens still have time to debate who may do the tracking.*

Location awareness will pervade the electronic world, thanks to ever more sophisticated radio transceivers, GPS chips, and government-backed emergency location initiatives like Enhanced-911 in the United States and Enhanced-112 in Europe. Cellphones, computers and cars will report position and unique identity in real time, with (or possibly without) owner consent. Lives will be saved, property recovered, and missing children found. But these benefits aren't the real reason that location awareness and reporting will spread to nearly every device. As described by science fiction author Vernor Vinge, it is going to happen because the capability will cost next to nothing as an integrated part of wireless technology. In the future, you can assume that almost any electronic device will be trackable, though citizens still have time to debate who may do the tracking.

The flood of information has to go someplace. Already databases fill with information about private individuals, from tax and medical records to credit ratings; from travel habits and retail purchases to which movies they recently downloaded on their TiVo personal video recorder. Yahoo's HotJobs recently began selling "self" background checks, offering job seekers a chance to vet their own personal, financial and legal data—the same information that companies might use to judge them. (True, a dating service that already screens for felons, recently expanded its partnership with database provider Rapsheets to review public records and verify a user's single status.) Data aggregators like Acxiom Corp., of Arkansas, or ChoicePoint, of Georgia, go even further, listing your car loans, outstanding liens and judgments, any professional or pilot or gun licenses, credit checks, and real estate you might own—all of it gathered from legal and open sources.

> *Whether the law officially allows it or not, can any effort by mere mortals prevent data from leaking?*

On the plus side, you'll be able to find and counter those rumors and slanderous untruths that can slash from the dark. The ability of others to harm you with lies may decline drastically. On the other hand, it will be simple for almost anybody using these methods to appraise the background of anyone else, including all sorts of unpleasant things that are inconveniently true. In other words, the rest of us will be able to do what elites (define them as you wish, from government to aristocrats to criminal masterminds) already can.

Some perceive this trend as ultimately empowering, while others see it as inherently oppressive. For example, activist groups from the ACLU [American Civil Liberties Union] to the Electronic Privacy Information Center call for European-style legislation aiming to seal the data behind perfect firewalls [Internet security software] into separate, isolated clusters that cannot cross-link or overlap. And in the short term, such efforts may prove beneficial. New database filters may help users find information they legitimately need while protecting personal privacy . . . for a while, buying us time to innovate for the long term.

> **" On the near horizon are wearable multimedia devices, with displays that blend into your sunglasses. "**

But we mustn't fool ourselves. No firewall, program or machine has ever been perfect, or perfectly implemented by fallible human beings. Whether the law officially allows it or not, can any effort by mere mortals prevent data from leaking? (And just one brief leak can spill a giant database into public knowledge, forever.) Cross-correlation will swiftly draw conclusions that are far more significant than the mere sum of the parts, adding up to a profoundly detailed picture of every citizen, down to details of personal taste. . . .

We tend to shrug over each other's harmless or opinionated eccentricities. But can that trait last very long when powerful groups scrutinize us, without being scrutinized back? In the long run, tolerance depends on the ability of any tolerated minority to enforce its right to be left alone. This is achieved assertively, not by hiding. And assertiveness is empowered by knowledge.

Wearable Surveillance Devices

The picture so far may seem daunting enough. Only now add a flood of new sensors. We have already seen the swift and inexpensive transformation of mere cellphones into a much more general, portable, electronic tool by adding the capabilities of a digital camera, audio recorder and PDA [personal digital assistant]. But have we fully grasped the implications, when any well-equipped pedestrian might swiftly transform into an ad hoc photojournalist—or peeping Tom—depending on opportunity or inclination?

On the near horizon are wearable multimedia devices, with displays that blend into your sunglasses, along with computational, data-storage and communications capabilities woven into the very clothes you wear. The term "augmented reality" will apply when these tools overlay your subjective view of the world with digitally supplied facts, directions or commentary. You will expect—and rely on—rapid answers to queries about any person or object in sight. In essence, this will be no different than querying your neuron-based memories about people in the village where you grew up. Only we had a million years to get used to tracking reputations that way. The new prosthetics that expand memory will prove awkward at first.

Today we worry about drivers who use cellphones at the wheel. Tomorrow will it be distracted pedestrians, muttering to no one as they walk? Will we grunt and babble while strolling along, like village idiots of yore?

> *Will you be better able to protect yourself if these technologies are banned (and thus driven underground) or regulated, with a free market that might offer us all pocket detectors, to catch scanners in the act?*

Maybe not. Having detected nerve signals near the larynx that are preparatory to forming words, scientists at NASA [National Aeronautics and Space Administration] Ames Research Center lately proposed *subvocal speech systems*—like those forecast in my 1989 novel *Earth*—that will accept commands without audible sounds. They would be potentially useful in spacesuits, noisy environments and to reduce the inevitable babble when we are all linked by wireless all the time.

Taking this trend in more general terms, *volition sensing* may pick up an even wider variety of cues, empowering you to converse, give commands, or participate in faraway events without speaking aloud or showing superficial signs.

Is this the pre-dawn of tech-mediated telepathy? It may be closer than you think. Advertising agencies are already funding research groups that use [brain scans] to study the immediate reactions of test subjects to marketing techniques and images. "We are crossing the chasm," said Adam Koval, chief operating officer of Thought Sciences, a division of Bright House, an Atlanta advertising and consulting firm whose clients include

Home Depot, Delta Airlines and Coca-Cola, "and bringing a new paradigm in analytic rigor to the world of marketing and advertising." Those who decry such studies face a tough burden, since all of the test subjects are paid volunteers. But how about when these methods leave the laboratory and hit the street? It is eerie to imagine a future when sensitive devices might scan your very thoughts when you pass by. Clearly there must be limits, only how? Will you be better able to protect yourself if these technologies are banned (and thus driven underground) or *regulated*, with a free market that might offer us all pocket detectors, to catch scanners in the act?

> *Soon, cyber-witnessing of public events, business deals, crimes and accidents will be routine.*

Microsoft recently unveiled Sensecam, a camera disguisable as jewelry that automatically records scores of images per hour from the wearer's point of view, digitally documenting an ongoing daily photo-diary. Such "Boswell machinery" may go far beyond egomania. For example, what good will your wallet do to a mugger when images of the crime are automatically broadcast across the Web? Soon, cyber-witnessing of public events, business deals, crimes and accidents will be routine. In movie parlance, you will have to assume that everybody you meet is carrying a "wire."

Looking Up

Meanwhile, you can be sure that military technologies will continue spinning off civilian versions, as happened with infrared night vision. Take "sniffers" designed to warn of environmental or chemical dangers on the battlefield. Soon, cheap and plentiful sensors will find their way into neighborhood storm drains, onto lampposts, or even your home faucet, giving rapid warnings of local pollution. Neighborhood or activist groups that create detector networks will have autonomous access to data rivaling that of local governments. Of course, a better-informed citizenry is sure to be more effective . . .

. . . and far more noisy.

The same spinoff effect has emerged from military development of inexpensive UAV [Unmanned Aerial Vehicle] battlefield reconnaissance drones. Some of the "toys" offered by Draganfly Innovations can cruise independently for more than an hour along a [satellite]-guided path, transmit 2.4 GHz digital video, then return automatically to the hobbyist owner. In other companies and laboratories, the aim is toward miniaturization, developing micro-flyers that can assist an infantry squad in an urban skirmish or carry eavesdropping equipment into the lair of a suspected terrorist. Again, civilian models are already starting to emerge. There may already be some in your neighborhood.

Cheap, innumerable eyes in the sky. One might envision dozens of potentially harmful uses . . . hundreds of beneficial ones . . . and millions of others in between ranging from irksome to innocuous . . . all leading toward a fundamental change in the way each of us relates to the horizon that so cruelly constrained the imagination of our ancestors. Just as baby boomers grew accustomed to viewing faraway places through the magical—though professionally mediated—channel of network television, so the next generation will simply assume that there is always another independent way to glimpse real-time events, either far away or just above the streets where they live.

> **❝ If our freedom depends on blinding the mighty, then we haven't a prayer. Fortunately, that isn't what really matters after all. ❞**

Should we push for yet another unenforceable law to guard our backyards against peeping Toms and their drone planes? Or perhaps we'd be better off simply insisting that the companies that make the little robot spies give us the means to trace them back to their nosy pilots. In other words, looking back may be a more effective way to protect privacy.

One might aim for reciprocal transparency using new technology. For example, Swiss researcher Marc Langheinrich's personal digital assistant application detects nearby sensors and then lists what kind of information they're collecting. At a more radical and polemical level, there is the *sousveillance* movement, led by University of Toronto professor Steve Mann.

Playing off "surveillance" (overlooking from above), Mann's coined term suggests that we should all get in the habit of looking from below, proving that we are sovereign and alert citizens down here, not helpless sheep. Mann contends that private individuals will be empowered to do this by new senses, dramatically augmented by wearable electronic devices.

We have skimmed over a wide range of new technologies, from RFID chips and stick-on penny cameras to new Internet address protocols and numerous means of biometric identification. From database mining and aggregation to sensors that detect chemical pollution or the volition to speak or act before your muscles get a chance to move. From omni-surveillance to universal localization. From eyes in the sky to those that may invade your personal space.

Note a common theme. Every device or function that's been described here serves to enhance some human sensory capability, from sight and hearing to memory. And while some may fret and fume, there is no historical precedent for a civilization refusing such prosthetics when they become available.

Such trends cannot be boiled down to a simple matter of good news or bad. While technologies of distributed vision may soon empower common folk in dramatic ways, giving a boost to participatory democracy by highly informed citizens, you will not hear that side of the message from most pundits, who habitually portray the very same technologies in a darker light, predicting that machines are about to destroy privacy, undermine values and ultimately enslave us.

In fact, the next century will be much too demanding for fixed perspectives. (Or rigid us-vs.-them ideologies.) Agility will be far more useful, plus a little healthy contrariness.

When in the company of reflexive pessimists—or knee-jerk optimists—the wise among us will be those saying . . . "Yes, but . . ."

Watching the Watchers

Which way will the pendulum of good and bad news finally swing?

We are frequently told that there is a fundamental choice to be made in a tragic trade-off between safety and freedom. While agents of the state, like [former] Attorney General John Ashcroft, demand new powers of surveillance—purportedly the better to protect us—champions of civil liberties such as the

ACLU warn against surrendering traditional constraints upon what the government is allowed to see. For example, they decry provisions of the PATRIOT Act that open broader channels of inspection, detection, search and data collection, predicting that such steps take us on the road toward Big Brother.

While they are right to fear such an outcome, they could not be more wrong about the specifics. As I discuss in greater detail elsewhere, the very idea of a *trade-off* between security and freedom is one of the most insidious and dismal notions I have ever heard—a perfect example of a devil's dichotomy. We modern citizens are living proof that people can and should have both. Freedom and safety, in fact, work together, not in opposition. Furthermore, I refuse to let anybody tell me that I must choose between liberty for my children and their safety! I refuse, and so should you.

As we've seen throughout this article, and a myriad other possible examples, there is no way that we will ever succeed in limiting the power of the elites to see and know. If our freedom depends on blinding the mighty, then we haven't a prayer.

Fortunately, that isn't what really matters after all. Moreover, John Ashcroft clearly knows it. By far the most worrisome and dangerous parts of the PATRIOT Act are those that remove the tools of supervision, allowing agents of the state to act secretly, without checks or accountability. (Ironically, these are the very portions that the ACLU and other groups have most neglected.)

In comparison, a few controversial alterations of procedure for search warrants are pretty minor. After all, appropriate levels of surveillance may shift as society and technology experience changes in a new century. (The Founders never heard of a wiretap, for example.)

But our need to watch the watchers will only grow.

It is a monopoly of vision that we need to fear above all else. So long as most of the eyes are owned by the citizens themselves, there will remain a chance for us to keep arguing knowledgeably among ourselves, debating and bickering, as sovereign, educated citizens should.

It will not be a convenient or anonymous world. Privacy may have to be redefined much closer to home. There will be a lot of noise.

But we will not drown under a rising tide of overwhelming technology. Keeping our heads, we will remain free to guide our ships across these rising waters—to choose a destiny of our own.

Organizations to Contact

The editors have compiled the following list of organizations concerned with the issues debated in this book. The descriptions are derived from materials provided by the organizations. All have publications or information available for interested readers. The list was compiled on the date of publication of the present volume; names, addresses, phone and fax numbers, and e-mail addresses may change. Be aware that many organizations take several weeks or longer to respond to inquiries, so allow as much time as possible.

The Berkman Center for Internet and Society
Harvard Law School, Baker House
1587 Massachusetts Ave., Cambridge, MA 02138
(617) 495-7547 • fax: (617) 495-7641
e-mail: cyber@law.harvard.edu
Web site: http://cyber.law.harvard.edu

This Internet studies research program seeks "to explore and understand cyberspace, its development, dynamics, norms, standards, and need or lack thereof for laws and sanctions." Berkman publishes a monthly e-mail newsletter, the *Filter*, and maintains online lectures, seminars, papers, and Web logs ("blogs") pertaining to digital media and piracy, online education, Internet pornography filters, Internet radio, Internet access in the developing world, and a host of other topics.

The Center for Democracy and Technology (CDT)
1634 Eye St., Suite 1100, Washington, DC 20006
(202) 637-9800 • fax: (202) 637-0968
e-mail: feedback@cdt.org • Web site: www.cdt.org

The CDT is a public policy advocacy group that takes libertarian positions on a number of issues in public policy, including Internet content restriction and privacy laws. It maintains an e-mail action alerts listserv, and publishes Internet-related news on its Web site.

Computer Professionals for Social Responsibility (CPSR)
PO Box 717, Palo Alto, CA 94302
(650) 322-3778 • fax: (650) 322-4748
e-mail: cpsr@cspr.org • Web site: www.cpsr.org

This public policy think tank advocates using computers to improve the quality of life, but works "to dispel popular myths about the infallibility of technological systems" and challenges "the assumption that technology alone can solve political and social problems." CPSR publishes the *CPSR Journal* quarterly and distributes a monthly e-mail newsletter, the *Compiler*. Its Web site provides many articles on the use of technology and the limitations of that technology.

Electronic Frontier Foundation (EFF)
454 Shotwell St., San Francisco, CA 94110-1914
(415) 436-9333 • fax: (415) 436-9993
e-mail: information@eff.org • Web site: www.eff.org

Founded in 1990, the EFF is one of the oldest and most influential Internet public policy organizations. It tends to take a civil libertarian position, funding lawsuits against Internet content restriction and surveillance and in favor of anonymity and file sharing. Its Web site hosts an online library of resources on thirty-seven different controversies in Internet public policy, and it distributes regular press releases and action alerts dealing with new cases and legislation.

Electronic Privacy Information Center (EPIC)
1718 Connecticut Ave. NW, Suite 200, Washington, DC 20009
(202) 483-1140 • fax: (202) 483-1248
Web site: www.epic.org

EPIC was founded in 1994 to defend civil liberties in the electronic frontier, particularly those pertaining to the First Amendment and the right to privacy. It publishes a biweekly online journal, the *EPIC Alert*, as well as numerous books and reports.

Free Software Foundation
59 Temple Pl., Suite 330, Boston, MA 02111-1307
(617) 542-5942 • fax: (617) 542-2652
e-mail: info@fsf.org • Web site: www.fsf.org

The GNU Project was founded in 1984 to create the free GNU computer operating system, a predecessor to Linux. It has evolved to become the Free Software Foundation, which supports authorship of "software unimpeded by private monopolies," First Amendment rights, and Internet privacy. The Web site links to articles, information about membership, and free software.

Internet Society (ISOC)
1775 Wiehle Ave., Suite 102, Reston, VA 20190-5108
(703) 326-9880 • fax: (703) 326-9881
e-mail: membership@isoc.org • Web site: www.isoc.org

With over 16,000 members in 180 countries, the Internet Society is dedicated to exploring solutions related to the structure, expansion, and sustainability of the Internet worldwide. ISOC has numerous articles, technical newsletters, and local small groups, as well as conferences and online discussion forums on its Web site.

Online Privacy Alliance
555 Thirteenth St. NW, Washington, DC 20004
(202) 637-5600
e-mail: webmaster@privacyalliance.org
Web site: www.privacyalliance.org

The Online Privacy Alliance encourages self-regulation in the pursuit of Internet privacy standards and enforcement of current laws regarding privacy. It has also focused, in recent years, on protecting the privacy of children online. It publishes regular news reports and position papers on issues affecting Internet privacy and provides guidelines free of charge for businesses interested in protecting the privacy of their customers.

People for Internet Responsibility (PFIR)
333 Ravenswood Ave., Menlo Park, CA 94025-3493
(818) 225-2800
e-mail: lauren@pfir.org • Web site: www.pfir.org

PFIR takes positions against spam, hacking, privacy violations, and other behavior that threatens Internet users. It also opposes most forms of Internet content restriction. PFIR hosts online forums, routinely publishes policy statements, and actively reports on Internet-related issues on its Web site.

Privacy International
Washington Office
1718 Connecticut Ave. NW, Suite 200, Washington, DC 20009
(202) 483-1217 • fax: (202) 483-1248
e-mail: privacyint@privacy.org
Web site: www.privacyinternational.org

Privacy International was founded in 1990 by representatives of over one hundred human rights organizations that were concerned about the erosion of privacy worldwide. In recent years it has focused much of its energy on Internet-related privacy issues, particularly those pertaining to cyber crime, data protection, and electronic surveillance. It routinely publishes news reports and position papers on privacy issues and occasionally sponsors international conferences dealing with privacy.

SafetyEd International
PO Box 511, Boulder Creek, CA 95006
e-mail: safetyed@safetyed.org • Web site: www.safetyed.org

SafetyEd is devoted to protecting children and teenagers from online harassment, stalking, exploitation, and privacy violations. It publishes numerous practical guides for parents, librarians, and teachers who are concerned about online safety issues.

Bibliography

Books

David Bell and Barbara M. Kennedy, eds. *The Cybercultures Reader.* London: Routledge, 2000.

Aaron Ben-Ze'ev *Love Online: Emotions on the Internet.* Cambridge, England: Cambridge University Press, 2004.

Stuart Biegel *Beyond Our Control? Confronting the Limits of Our Legal System in the Age of Cyberspace.* Cambridge, MA: MIT Press, 2003.

Joshua Gay, ed. *Free Software, Free Society: Selected Essays of Richard M. Stallman.* Boston: Free Software Foundation, 2002.

Adam M. Joinson *Understanding the Psychology of Internet Behaviour: Virtual Worlds, Real Lives.* New York: Palgrave Macmillan, 2003.

Ray Kurzweil *The Age of Spiritual Machines: When Computers Exceed Human Intelligence.* New York: Penguin Putnam, 2000.

Lawrence Lessig *Free Culture: How Big Media Uses Technology and the Law to Lock Down Culture and Control Creativity.* New York: Penguin, 2004.

Lawrence Lessig *The Future of Ideas: The Fate of the Commons in a Connected World.* New York: Random House, 2001.

Jessica Litman *Digital Copyright: Protecting Intellectual Property on the Internet.* Amherst, NY: Prometheus Books, 2000.

Howard Rheingold *Smart Mobs: The Next Social Revolution.* New York: Basic Books, 2003.

Siva Vaidhyanathan *The Anarchist in the Library: How the Clash Between Freedom and Control Is Hacking the Real World and Crashing the System.* New York: Basic Books, 2004.

Siva Vaidhyanathan *Copyrights and Copywrongs: The Rise of Intellectual Property and How It Threatens Creativity.* New York: NYU Press, 2003.

Periodicals

Hampton Auld "Filters Work: Get Over It," *American Libraries*, February 2003.

Kevin Baker	"Copy Wrong: Internet Piracy and Dickens and Melville," *American Heritage*, June/July 2004.
Jeffrey Barlow	"Surfing with Good and Evil," *Journal of Education, Community, and Values*, April/May 2004.
Celeste Biever	"Logging On Could Require a Swipe Card," *New Scientist*, February 25, 2004.
Marcel Bullinga	"The Internet of the Future: To Control or Be Controlled," *Futurist*, May/June 2002.
Christianity Today	"Good Idea, Fallible Filters," February 19, 2001.
Sean Ebare	"Digital Music and Subculture: Sharing Files, Sharing Styles," *First Monday*, February 2, 2004.
Susan L. Gerhart	"Do Web Search Engines Suppress Controversy?" *First Monday*, January 5, 2004.
Neil Gershenfeld, Raffi Krikorian, and Danny Cohen	"The Internet of Things," *Scientific American*, October 2004.
Thomas Goetz	"Open Source Everywhere," *Wired*, November 2003.
Michael H. Goldhaber	"The Mentality of *Homo Interneticus:* Some Ongian Postulates," *First Monday*, June 7, 2004.
Steven Johnson	"Internet-Era Democracy," *Discover*, January 2004.
Ken Jordan, Jan Hauser, and Steven Foster	"The Augmented Social Network: Building Identity and Trust into the Next-Generation Internet," *First Monday*, August 4, 2003.
Shanthi Kalathil and Taylor C. Boas	"Open Networks, Closed Regimes: The Impact of the Internet on Authoritarian Rule," *First Monday*, January 6, 2003.
Nancy Kranich	"Why Filters Won't Protect Children or Adults," *Library Administration & Management*, Winter 2004.
John Logie	"A Copyright Cold War? The Polarized Rhetoric of the Peer-to-Peer Debates," *First Monday*, July 7, 2003.
Brendan Luyt	"Who Benefits from the Digital Divide?" *First Monday*, August 2, 2004.
Chris Preimesberger	"Commentary: Online Voting? Of Course It Can Work," *IT Manager's Journal*, February 17, 2004.
Larry Press	"Wireless Internet Connectivity for Developing Nations," *First Monday*, September 1, 2003.
Indhu Rajagopal and Nis Bojin	"Globalization of Prurience: The Internet and the Degradation of Women and Children," *First Monday*, January 5, 2004.
Katharine Sarikakis	"Ideology and Policy: Notes on the Shaping of the Internet," *First Monday*, August 2, 2004.

Claude Solnik — "Politics on the Web: A Brief History," *Long Island (N.Y.) Business News*, July 30, 2004.

Jörgen S. Svensson and Frank Bannister — "Pirates, Sharks, and Moral Crusaders: Social Control in Peer-to-Peer Networks," *First Monday*, June 7, 2004.

Siva Vaidhyanathan — "The State of Copyright Activism," *First Monday*, April 5, 2004.

Gary Wolf — "Weapons of Mass Mobilization," *Wired*, September 2004.

Index

106